# DÉCOUPAGE
## & PAINTED FURNITURE
### *for beautiful interiors*

# DÉCOUPAGE
# & PAINTED FURNITURE
## for beautiful interiors

### RUBENA GRIGG

David & Charles

*TULIPS, VIOLAS AND ROSES decorate mostly junk-shop buys*

A DAVID & CHARLES BOOK

Copyright © Text, designs and illustrations Rubena Grigg 1995
© Photographs David & Charles 1995

First published 1995

A catalogue record for this book is available from the British Library.

ISBN 0 7153 0184 5

Book design by Diana Knapp
Photography by Di Lewis

Typeset by Ace Filmsetting Ltd, Frome, Somerset
and printed in Italy by Lego Vicenza
for David & Charles
Brunel House  Newton Abbot  Devon

# CONTENTS

# INTRODUCTION

My early childhood was spent in the depths of Lincolnshire where I learned to appreciate a naturalistic way of life and the simple pleasures of the countryside. As an only child I spent many hours sketching, drawing and painting and, I am ashamed to admit, dressing up a very unwilling cat! Toy theatres fascinated me; papier mâché and cutting collages, modelling with Plasticine and clay.

Only in the last 10 years have I begun to realize the lasting influence of those creative days and the importance of 'play'. Having reverted to a similar lifestyle the ideas are flowing again, expressed now in the form of découpage. I do hope that something in this book will rekindle a similar flame for you, and give you many hours of creative pleasure.

Découpage is a fascinating art and delightful hobby. Meaning 'cut out' (from the French *découper*) it involves carefully cutting out paper images and pasting them on to almost any surface, before applying varnish to give the impression of hand-painting or inlay.

Découpage is enjoying a tremendous revival. The beauty of it is that it calls for no artistic talent: as this book will show, after the simple basic techniques have been mastered all that is needed to create the most spectacular results is an eye for colour and design and a little patience.

It is very satisfying to transform shabby household items or junk-shops finds into beautiful decorative pieces, and immensely pleasurable to be able to design and decorate a room in one's own choice of colour and motif, incorporating fabric and texture into the scheme.

Throughout the book paint-finishes are used as background for the découpage. You may be inspired by a favourite piece of porcelain or a painting, by the flowers on a fabric or the colours in a beautiful rug. Like me you may draw your inspiration from the countryside; the possibilities are endless and each design will be a reflection of your unique personality. I have included a wide variety of ideas which should appeal to beginners and more advanced découpers alike.

There are over 70 projects and ideas ranging from small decorative pieces to large items of furniture. Here you will find découpage projects for every room in the house: a coffee-table for the sitting-room, screens of varying size and description, Victorian and Edwardian tolewear for the conservatory and a sumptuously romantic headboard decorated with cherubs and swags of roses. I have combined the use of paint and découpage on an elegant demi-lune table with sweet little floral cameos. Throughout the book you will find many projects using tin and tolewear, which over the years has become a speciality of mine.

Découpage adds interest to many new items and can enhance old ones, particularly if they have become marked or stained. Subjects may be small or large, the larger the surface the more scope there is for producing bold design work.

Chapter 1 provides all the information you will need to get started, with clear, illustrated step-by-step instructions showing you exactly how to prepare, decorate and varnish your découpage project. We also show you how to achieve various background paint-finishes, and demonstrate techniques to transform otherwise ordinary pieces of furniture with hand-painted ribbons, leaves, bows, ropes and tassels, and by applying craquelure and antique finishes. There is also a section devoted to problem solving with helpful hints and tips. A list of suppliers will be found on pages 142–3.

There is no shortage of good-quality wrapping paper from which to create your own stunning designs so choose your object, pick up the scissors and start snipping!

*HYDRANGEAS brings this simple jug and bowl to life*

◆

# 1

# GETTING STARTED

$T$he materials for découpage are easy to find, and unlike many decorative arts, fairly cheap. Most items are available locally, but addresses of specialist suppliers are listed on pages 142–3.

◆  ◆  ◆  ◆

### ◆ *materials* ◆

The following materials will enable you to complete most of the projects in the book. Any additional supplies required are listed in the individual project sections.

**INITIAL PREPARATION**
A supply of 100 grade sandpaper to sand your items before applying the undercoat, and fine 240 grade glasspaper or 00 grade flour paper to rub down subsequent coats of paint and varnish for a smooth finish.

**UNDERCOATING**
A small tin of acrylic primer undercoat or red oxide metal primer for tinware will suffice for most projects.

**BACKGROUND COLOUR**
A small tin of vinyl silk emulsion paint in a colour of your choice.

**BRUSHES**
2.5cm (1 inch) paint brushes of medium quality that will

not shed many hairs are used for painting and varnishing. Keep a separate brush for varnishing. You will also need a No. 4 artist's brush for gilt decoration.

**PAPER**
Good-quality wrapping paper with plenty of definition, prints or hand-coloured photocopies. Paper must be printed on one side only otherwise the pattern on the reverse will show through when you apply the varnish.

**SCISSORS**
A pair of small, pointed and very sharp scissors, such as Wilkinson's straight manicure, which can be purchased from most chemists. You should not use a scalpel or craft knife as these will scuff the edges of the paper and make incisions which are too angular. They are also much slower to use.

**GLUE**
You will need ready-mixed water-soluble extra-strong

wallpaper adhesive and a small glue brush.

### CLEANING
Use a small sponge or kitchen paper, dampened slightly with water, to clean off excess glue from your work.

### GILDING
To paint antique gold decoration you will need small tubes of Gold and Raw Umber artists' acrylic paint. Use a No. 4 artist's brush to apply the gilt finish.

### TAKCLOTH
A varnish-impregnated cloth for removing dust particles before each coat of varnish is applied. 'Takrag' is one of the more popular brand names in the UK.

### VARNISH
Varnish has a tendency to develop a deep yellowish tinge as successive coats are applied, which will alter the colours of your work, so use the palest craft varnish you can find.

Throughout the book I have used a semi-matt polyurethane lacquer which is available in many different sizes. Fast drying water-based acrylic varnishes are not suitable for découpage. They are fine when only four or five coats are used to protect a surface, but with the many applications required in découpage their appear-ance becomes milky. It is essential to use a good-quality pale varnish or polyurethane lacquer in gloss, semi-matt or pale eggshell, and occasionally flat finish. Gloss is the most hard-wearing, matt the least, so for a durable matt finish, use gloss for all but the top two coats, which can be matt. For makers and suppliers see pages 142–3.

### BRUSH CLEANING
Use white spirit or a proprietary brush-cleaner to clean your brushes after using oil-based paint or varnish before washing them out in soap and water. If using spirit-based products such as shellac, clean up using methylated spirit. Always read and follow the manufacturer's instructions.

### ACCESSORIES
You will need a suitable *board* (or boards for larger projects) for pasting on the glue: offcuts of melamine, white-faced hardboard or the smooth side of ordinary hardboard (all available from DIY shops) are suitable; a *craft knife* to lift pasted cutouts to adjust their position on the surface of your work; a piece of *white chalk* for drawing round the shape of the cutout design; screw-top *jars* or clean *cartons* with lids (eg margarine tubs) make ideal containers for white spirit and water respectively.

(*NOTE*   always store solvents in glass containers.)

## SAFETY PRECAUTIONS

◆   Work in a well-ventilated area when using varnishes and solvents. Breathing fumes can lead to unconsciousness and permanent damage. Wear a respiratory mask to protect against the inhalation of fumes.

◆   Take suitable fire precautions if working with inflammable products.

◆   Always read the manufacturer's instructions.

◆   Wear thin all-purpose gloves when using methylated spirits, white spirit or turpentine, especially if you have a sensitive skin or are prone to allergies. (These are available in multi-packs from most supermarkets.)

◆   Keep all materials out of reach of children. Use food containers with care: pretty colours in familiar containers are very tempting to a child.

◆   A cheap paper dust mask will protect against inhalation of dust and paint particles, particularly when using a power sander.

◆   Old paint contains lead: remember that poisons can be absorbed by skin contact as well as by inhalation and swallowing.

◆   Most wallpaper pastes contain fungicides which can cause skin irritation and dermatitis. Rinse fingers frequently and do not touch your face while working with glue.

# First Project –
# A SET OF TABLEMATS

*There is no substitute for 'learning by doing' and this simple project will teach you the basics of preparation, application and finishing, at the same time creating a beautiful addition to your dining-table.*
*For a first attempt these octagonal mats offer a lovely simple shape and a good even surface on which to work. The colour I have chosen for the painted background is a gorgeous rich country green which will show up flowers and fruit to their full advantage. It is important to use a darker background until you have become a little more experienced at cutting and also to choose a paper with a similar background colour.*
*A whole variety of designs look attractive. The design can be in the form of a garland or overlaid to cover more of the surface. The flowers can be in small groups or they can appear to 'grow' from the base of the mat; alternatively the paper cutouts can be arranged in a central posy. Whatever design you choose, try to ensure that it looks attractive from every viewpoint.*
*The moulded edges are painted in a soft antique gold which frames the design and gives a really professional finish. Once you have completed the first mat you will be so thrilled with the results that you will be spurred on to make a set. Each one can be totally different in layout (so you will not become bored!), but by using the same paper they will obviously be a set.*

## ◆ materials list ◆

In addition to the items listed on pages 8–9 you will need:

A number of identically shaped MDF or
    wooden table mats

Sufficient self-adhesive suede or baize to cover
    the underside of each mat

## ◆ preparation ◆

*1*  Paint the mats with acrylic primer undercoat and

allow to dry. Sand the edges and surface of the mats using 100 grade sandpaper. Remove dust with a tak-cloth, then apply a second coat of paint and allow to dry. If the edges still feel rough, sand again. Over-paint with your chosen colour, applying at least two coats until the finish looks perfect.

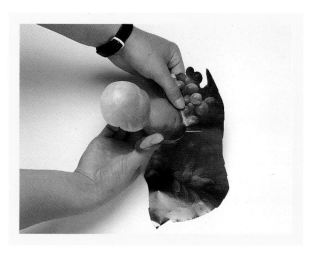

*2*  Cut out your motifs holding the scissors in a relaxed fashion. Always cut in the same direction for a natural flowing line around the edges. (Avoid square petals please!) If possible turn the paper and not the scissors as you cut in and out of petals and leaves. Once you have mastered the technique you will never look back.

*OCTAGONAL TABLEMATS decorated with fruits and flowers cut from a horticultural diary; the
grapes and peaches were cut from wrapping paper*

Until you are used to cutting, it is a good idea to cut a little deeper into the pattern rather than leave any background showing. Try to hold the scissors under-neath the paper (see picture); it will be less likely to tear and will not reveal a white cut edge when stuck down on the mat.

To cut out a piece that is completely encircled by your motif make a small incision with the point of the scissors and resume cutting from underneath as before. If this is impractical, cut through a stem or leaf, or around a petal following the line where it will be less noticeable. The cut edges can be butted together so that the join is invisible when it is stuck down. Complicated curling stems can be cut through in one or two places and carefully butted together to become a complete stem again when pasted on to the work.

When you have cut out a good pile of paper motifs you can begin to make the design. Play around with the cutouts on the surface of your object until the picture you create is well balanced in shape and colour.

*3* When you have placed the finalized design on to the mat it is helpful to chalk carefully around the edge of the design, holding it in place with the palm of your hand as you do so, so that the shape is marked on the surface.

This gives a good indication of where to replace the cutouts when you have pasted them. The chalk marks can easily be removed with a damp sponge or paper towel later on. If you have decided to overlay the pieces of paper, when you have chalked around the edges, remove the uppermost cutouts to reveal the underneath shapes and chalk around those too.

### • *creating a design* •

For me, creating a design is the most exciting part. For our tablemat project there are several options:

• MAKE A GARLAND to encircle the tablemat, slightly overlapping the flowers and leaves as they would in a real flower arrangement; this is known as overlaying

• CREATE A POSY in the mat's centre
• PLACE MOTIFS in each angle
• 'GROW' THE FLOWERS from the base of the tablemat. This design has the obvious drawback that it needs to be viewed the right way up to be appreciated fully
• USE A MIXTURE OF STYLES. So long as they all originate from the same paper, they will make a delightful set and be the talking point of any meal

### • *applying the glue* •

*1* You will need a pasting board(s), ready mixed adhesive, glue brush, craft knife, small sponge, kitchen paper and a container of water.

*2* Select the first motif (if you are overlaying take the underneath piece first); turn it face down on to the board and brush on the glue from the centre outwards, spreading it evenly over the entire surface and ensuring that the edges are covered. Lift, using your craft knife if necessary, and reposition within the chalk marks on the surface of the work.

*3* Eliminate any air bubbles, blemishes and excess glue with your fingers, dipping them in water if you find it helps (there is less likelihood of tearing the paper with wet fingers). Work from the centre of the motif using a rolling movement of the fingers and carefully wipe away excess glue with damp kitchen paper. If your fingers become sticky, rinse occasionally in water as they will remove the print from the surface of the paper. When the cutout is absolutely flat, press the edges down. Remember, glue may contain toxins and skin irritants.

4  When your decoration is finished let it dry out.

5  You now need to remove any dried glue from the surface of the work. For this you will need a bowl of warm water and a small sponge (or kitchen paper). Dampen the sponge slightly and begin to clean the glue from the surface of the paper design working gently from the centre of the cutouts to the edges. Then clean off the background taking care not to scuff the edges of the paper. If there are any loose edges stick them down now and clean up carefully straight away.

6  Tilt the work towards a light source to check that all the glue has been removed and the work is clean and ready for varnishing.

### • *gilding with antique gold* •

Fill the base of a glass jar or clean carton with water and squeeze a small amount of Gold and Raw Umber artists' acrylic paint on to the lid. Mix together a portion of the colours with a little water making it quite dark for the first application.

Brush the first coat of antique gold on to the rim of the work, always working in the same direction (going back will remove the gold particles). Approximately four coats is usually required to get a good depth; lighten each coat gradually by increasing the proportion of Gold in the paint mix until the colour is to your taste. Acrylic paint is water-based and will dry quickly, so you will be able to apply successive coats almost continuously.

Take great care to avoid getting paint on your fingers and transferring it to the surface of the work. Have some damp kitchen roll at the ready to wipe it off immediately, otherwise the gold particles will be illuminated by the varnish later on! The antique gold will 'frame' your work setting off the design and giving it a professional finish. Leave to dry before varnishing.

### • *varnishing* •

1  Use a takcloth to remove all traces of dust from the surface of the work. Wipe the edges first, then the surface, working in one direction.

2  After stirring the varnish, apply the first coat sparingly so that it does not become absorbed by the paper design and thereby discolour it. Apply a thin coat, brushing it on around the edges first, then across the surface of the work spreading the varnish evenly, finally brushing it in one direction using the tip of the brush. Leave to dry for six to eight hours (or longer if recommended by the manufacturer – the time will also depend upon the air temperature in the room).

3  Subsequent coats of varnish may be applied more liberally but the art is to spread it out quickly and evenly, remove any excess from the brush by wiping it on the side of a jar or tin, and brush the varnish again in one direction, clearing the brush every so often and gently tickling the varnished surface with the tip of the brush. Repeat this until the air bubbles have been brushed out and the surface is as perfect as you can get it. *Remember to wipe the surface of the work with the Takcloth first to remove dust before applying the varnish.*

4  If the brush sheds hairs or there are visible pieces of fluff in the wet varnish, remove them with your finger or work them to the side with the brush. Once they are removed, brush out the varnish in one direction again for a good finish.

5  Always leave varnish to dry thoroughly before takking and applying another coat. The number of coats required will depend on the thickness of the paper used and the amount of overlaying in the design: the thicker the design, the more layers of varnish will be required to 'lose' the edges. Approximately 10 coats should be sufficient for items of tinware unless the design is overlaid a great deal.

6 When at least 10 coats have been applied, and provided the edges of the paper are lost beneath the varnish giving it a wonderful depth and hiding any 'stuck on' look (if not continue varnishing), take a *fresh* sheet of the finest grade glass or flour paper and gently rub the surface to remove any visible hairs and pieces of gritty dust that inevitably build up. Take care not to catch any painted edges. Do not be alarmed when the surface looks scratched, this will disappear with the next coat of varnish. Remember to use the takcloth to remove the particles of dust from sanding before the next application of varnish.

**Never** attempt to sand your work until at least 10 coats of varnish have been applied. If you do there is a strong possibility that you will rub through the surface of the paper, especially the edges. Tinware should not normally require sanding unless the varnish runs. (See page 27 for some useful advice on solving découpage problems.)

The takcloth is vital in obtaining a dust free surface on which to work. If dust reappears on the surface at any stage, sand gently again to remove, and repeat the process. The final two coats must be absolutely perfect otherwise the effect will be spoilt completely. Leave to dry for a day or two for the varnish to harden.

Objects that will take a lot of wear, such as trays, tablemats or coffee-tables, should be given many more layers of varnish. Gloss is the most hard-wearing and can be used to build up the layers, changing to semi-matt for the final three or four coats. For tablemats, trays and decorative objects which may be placed on furniture, an adhesive backed baize or suede can be cut to shape and applied to the underside of the work when all the varnishing is completely dry.

## VARNISHING TIPS!

- Varnish yellows in direct sunlight particularly on pale colours. I favour Mylands No. 8 semi-matt clear polyurethane varnish which I find the least yellowing (see suppliers list on pages 142–3)
- Never immerse varnished objects in water as immersion may damage and discolour the varnish
- Never shake a tin of varnish as this will create innumerable air bubbles; always stir it instead
- Semi-matt varnish must always be stirred to bring the cloudiness up from the bottom of the tin
- Keep some brushes specifically for varnishing
- Never wear wool to varnish; an old cotton shirt is best
- Always work in a well-ventilated area
- Always follow the manufacturer's instructions

# SOME MORE BASICS

*In addition to the skills you have learned while completing your tablemat project, there are a number of other basic techniques with which you must be familiar in order to complete the projects in the remaining chapters. These are detailed below, followed by a few helpful hints which may help you out of a difficult situation.*

## Preparation of wood

### • *complete stripping* •

Unless they are new, most wooden items will be covered with paint, varnish or some other finish which may require removal before you can begin work. If you wish to strip a piece of furniture completely it may be better to use a professional furniture stripping company who

◆

usually collect and deliver at a reasonable price. This is well worth while for the amount of effort it saves on large items. However, there is no reason why most pieces cannot be done by hand. A proprietary stripper such as Nitromors is the answer – do follow the manufacturer's instructions and safety precautions and wear thick gloves. Remove handles, knobs and fittings first if possible. Any filling or repairs should also be carried out at this stage. Once stripped, treat the piece as for new wood omitting the sanding sealer (below). If you own a power sander your work will be cut by half.

### ◆ painted surfaces ◆

If you intend repainting the item, use 100 grade sandpaper to rub down the entire surface, working in the same direction as the grain in the wood. This will create a 'key' on which to repaint. Remove dust with a damp cloth and apply two coats of acrylic primer undercoat; allow to dry between coats. Always feel the surface by running your fingers over it. Sand down any rough patches with 100 grade sandpaper, paying particular attention to the edges and tops of drawers etc. Apply two or three thin coats of top colour until a dense all-over cover is achieved.

### ◆ stained wood ◆

Sand the surfaces with 100 grade sandpaper working in the same direction as the grain in the wood. Stain 'bleeds' into paint and a barrier has to be created between the two. Coat the item with either a flat matt varnish (which

may take up to six hours to dry), or with two coats of shellac varnish thinned with a little methylated spirit. Shellac varnish is fast drying and it should be possible to apply the second coat in half an hour (keep your brush soft in a small amount of methylated spirit in a *glass* jar). When the barrier varnish is dry, paint in the normal way with undercoat and topcoat.

### ◆ new wood ◆

Run your fingers over the surface to find any rough patches and rub down with 100 grade sandpaper as before. Remove dust. If there are knots in the wood, apply sanding sealer, otherwise apply the first coat of acrylic primer undercoat and allow to dry. If the surface feels anything but smooth, sand the entire piece using 180 grade sandpaper and repeat the process. Apply two or three undercoats letting it dry between coats. Apply sufficient coats of top colour for a dense all-over cover.

### ◆ MDF – medium density ◆ fibreboard

Rub down the entire surface with 100 grade sandpaper, paying particular attention to mouldings and edges. Remove dust and apply a coat of acrylic primer undercoat. Leave to dry, then run your fingers over the surface and if it has roughened anywhere, rub it down again using 180 grade sandpaper. Apply another two coats of primer undercoat allowing it to dry between coats. Apply sufficient coats of top colour for a dense all-over cover.

## Preparation of tinware

### ◆ materials list ◆

Red oxide metal primer
2.5cm (1 inch) paintbrush
White spirit for cleaning up
Kitchen paper
Rubber gloves
Jar with lid for white spirit
Suitable wire brush (these are available
    in various shapes and sizes
    from DIY and hardware stores)
Car body-filler for filling holes

*HIGH-NECKED EDWARDIAN jug, before preparation, with materials*

*SOME OF THE ITEMS used in the projects, before preparation and decoration*

Many metal junk-shop buys are perfect subjects for découpage, but they are often found covered in rust and chipped enamel. This situation must be rectified before you can set about beautifying them.

The term 'tinware' covers a whole range of metal including white, blue and green enamel, tin, toleware, zinc, galvanized iron and aluminium. With the exception of zinc and galvanized iron (dealt with separately on page 18), tinware is easy to prepare. Removing rust can be rather messy, but should you find something unusually rare, wonderfully shaped or particularly pretty which is covered in rust and you are keen to do it, there is no choice but to don a pair of rubber gloves and an apron, take your wire brush in hand and get cracking!

*1* Brush off all the loose rust from the surface concentrating especially on seams in the metal, around the necks of jugs, joins where handles and spouts meet the main body, the edges of lids (which are often battered), spouts and around hinges.

*2* Give the tinware a good scrub. Clear the decks around the sink area and wash it thoroughly using a stiff brush or scouring sponge and a cream cleaner. Washing-up liquid on its own will not do the job of removing years of grime, grease, coal dust, paint spatters, bird droppings, discoloration from Granny's ginger wine, and so forth. If possible turn the piece upside down in a warm place to dry, but beware of dust if drying outside.

*3* Once the tinware is completely dry, fill any holes or huge chips with a car body-filler (time-consuming, but essential if the vessel is to contain liquid – otherwise 'dried flowers only'!).

Your piece is now as good as new in découpage terms, and the instructions hereafter apply to new and restored tinware alike.

*4* Paint the piece with red oxide metal primer using an old, used or cheap brush as there are tiny iron particles in the red oxide which are almost impossible to remove even with the most careful cleaning. It is a good idea to set aside a brush specifically for this purpose. Apply evenly, spreading it over the surface as it does tend to run. Some people find this a difficult medium to work with at first, but you will soon get the hang of it. I use it in preference to an ordinary metal primer as the density of cover is better and a second coat may be applied within an hour. Remember to stir well and follow the manufacturer's instructions. Allow to dry for approximately 30 minutes in a warm environment before applying the second coat. Leave overnight to dry out.

AFTER THE FIRST STAGES *of preparation, the jug is cleaned and painted with red-oxide metal primer. On the inside, this type of jug needs painting only down to the neck seam*

The red oxide primer retards rust to a certain extent and also gives a good 'key' on which to paint, creating an even surface and filling in any pits in the metal. Even a brand new piece of enamel needs this 'key' or else the paint will slip and slide and it will take you twice as long to do.

When painting tall Victorian and Edwardian jugs which have narrow necks, the oxide need be taken down only as far as the neck seam on the inside, leaving the remainder (which is unnoticeable) unpainted. Wide-necked jugs and items without lids should be painted on the inside or the final result will be rather ugly. It is, however, advisable to leave the inner surfaces of breadbins, canisters, etc unpainted if they are to be used for storing food since ingesting red oxide paint is very unhealthy!

For the next stage there are two options open depending upon the topcoat you have chosen.

5a   If you are using a *pale colour* the next step is to undercoat with white acrylic primer undercoat which is

fast drying, gives good cover and is water based. Paint at least two coats, applying additional coats if necessary until the surface is perfectly covered. Now apply two or three coats of your chosen acrylic emulsion.

APPLYING THE FIRST COAT *of acrylic primer undercoat to a red-oxided tinware bucket. Note that the inside is fully visible so it would look better covered completely with red oxide and two coats of paint, but this is optional*

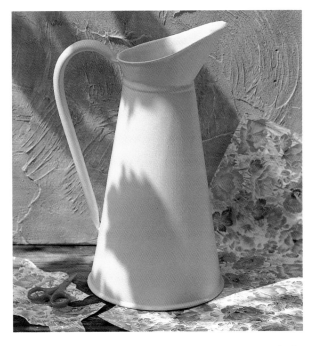

THE FULLY PREPARED JUG, *with four coats of cream vinyl silk emulsion on top of the primer undercoat and red oxide. The jug is now ready for its découpage decoration*

*5b* If you have decided on a *dark colour* there is no need to undercoat unless you wish to. Instead, apply three or four coats of emulsion until the surface is perfectly covered. Use either vinyl matt or vinyl silk emulsion. Occasionally a water-based paint refuses to adhere to a red-oxide primed surface, behaving as if the surface were greasy. A good tip is to add a little washing-up liquid to the paint. **Never** use eggshell paint as it seems to be incompatible with the adhesive and all your hard work in cutting an amazing design will be wasted when the paper dries and leaves the painted surface!

Vinyl matt emulsion is available in 250ml tins in a huge variety of colours; vinyl silk is available in 500ml tins and has the advantage of a slight sheen making it possible to move the pasted paper motifs on the surface until they are in their correct position. It is therefore recommended for beginners. Clean brushes after use according to the paint manufacturer's instructions.

### ◆ *zinc and galvanized iron* ◆

Zinc items are usually coated with a greasy flux which must be removed with degreasing fluid before priming. Degreasing fluid can be purchased from car accessory shops. Paint the liquid on to the object covering the entire surface and wash it off immediately. (If degreasing fluid is unavailable, an alternative is to soak the item in hot soapy water.) Rinse well, leave to dry thoroughly and it will be ready to paint with red oxide metal primer.

New galvanized iron tends to resist oxide and paint. The best preparatory treatment is to leave it outside to weather and lose its shine. However, I have painted new buckets with two coats of shellac varnish before red-oxiding with successful results. There is a special primer available for galvanized metal, but it is lead based and therefore in my opinion should be avoided at all costs.

## *Paint finishes*

Many items are made more attractive by the addition of an abstract, painted pattern applied to the background before découpage. Such additions are known as paint-finishes. (See, for example, the photographs on pages 83, 104 and 106.)

With the exception of the decorative box on page 40 which has a fan finish, every paint-finish in the book has been accomplished by using natural sea-sponge. It can be used open loosely so that its shape and pattern become the design on the surface of the work – a broken paint-finish. Alternatively, it can be squeezed in the hand and dabbed closely to give a flowing movement on the surface, a technique which I call 'close sponging'.

The most delicate colours can be used together very successfully; a pale cream on white or white sponged on to deep cream looks not only subtle but sophisticated. By using a dark colour as a base and sponging on the same colour lightened several shades by adding white to it is also very effective. Sponging on three complementary colours together (e.g. Venetian Red, Payne's Grey and Raw Umber, lightened with white in places) onto a base colour of black will give a rich finish with great depth (see the mirror frame opposite). Experiment with colour and techniques – you'll be amazed!

Sponging can be as sparse or as busy as you wish, but should never look regimented. Bright colours appear mellower under many layers of varnish or an antique finish.

*A SECTION OF A MIRROR frame showing sponging using three complementary colours – Venetian Red, Payne's Grey and Raw Umber – on a black background lightened in places with white and touched with gold*

**Emulsion glazes** To produce lovely soft translucent colours it is necessary to mix an emulsion glaze using equal parts of Unibond/PVA adhesive and emulsion paint mixed with 1:4 parts water. This medium is low odour, fast drying and keeps well in a screw-top jar or airtight container.

In several recipes for emulsion glazes throughout the book I have suggested using matchpots or 250ml tins of emulsion from the mixed-to-order Dulux Definitions, Sanderson Matchmaker or other ranges as alternatives to artist's acrylics. Both mediums are excellent, but if you can find the required colour in ready-mixed form elsewhere you may as well use it in the glaze – it is cheaper, and you will have some left over for future use.

### ◆ *sponging* ◆

### ◆ *materials list* ◆

Natural sea-sponge
Kitchen paper
Clean container with lid
Small tin Unibond/PVA adhesive
Matt emulsion paint (coloured) or white
    emulsion mixed with artists' acrylic colours
    of your choice
Old spoon for measuring
Water to mix

SPONGING SAMPLES: *(top) yellow on white – the right-hand section also has white on top of the yellow; (middle) yellow painted background sponged white and when dry sponged yellow over the white; (bottom) pale green background close sponged with white and green together*

◆

**Simple sponging** Measure out equal parts of Unibond/ PVA and emulsion paint mixed 1:4 with water. Combine the PVA and paint mixture in a carton to form an emulsion glaze. Sponge on as described above. For two, three and four colour sponging mix the emulsion glaze in a wide carton and use the lid as a palette, adding acrylic tube colours, emulsion, or a mixture of both to achieve your desired colour.

**Parchment finish** For the look of parchment the background is cream *vinyl silk* with a few veins of Soft Ochre, Raw Sienna and white. For a more intense colour I have used the following four colours for sponging: (1) Yellow Ochre (acrylic); (2) Acid Yellow (emulsion or acrylic); (3) minute amount of Raw Umber or Payne's Grey (acrylic); (4) white (emulsion or acrylic).

Mix the emulsion glaze as before using cream vinyl silk. Dip the sponge into the glaze first and then into one or two of the colours and apply to the surface. Close sponge diagonally and create interesting patches of movement and colour building the pattern and density gradually. Clean the sponge thoroughly after use.

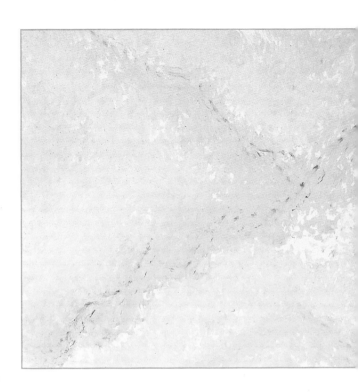

BUILDING UP A SPONGED *Acid Yellow finish, which will be toned down with white and cream*

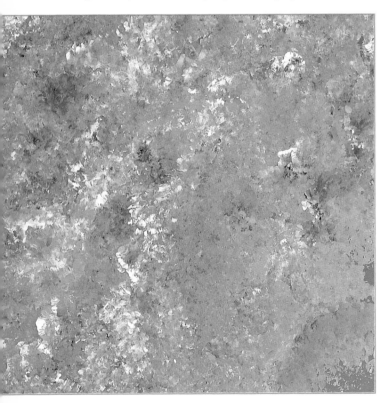

BUILDING UP SEVERAL *sponged colours to create the polished- slate effect for the coffee table on page 78*

BUILDING UP A SPONGED *ochre parchment finish*

◆

FAN FINISHES *As the sample board illustrates, it is possible to produce many different patterns using two or more complementary colours or those of the same shade. These effects are painted with a No. 6 fan brush by dipping each side of the brush into a different colour and by pulling the brush toward you along the surface, then returning to pull it through the colours. Experiment by wiggling and turning the brush to find your own techniques*

◆

# Hand-painted finishing touches

Hand-painted decoration can add a lovely finishing touch to your work. I think these look best in gold as described below, but you can experiment with other colours if you wish. Practise on paper first! When decorating objects, keep a damp sponge or kitchen roll handy so that any mistakes can be quickly erased.

---

### ♦ materials list ♦

Small tubes of artists' acrylics in Gold and Raw Umber or two colours of the same family, one dark and one light
Artist's brush (No. 4 is an average size, but it will depend upon the piece of work)
Wide carton with lid
Kitchen paper
Water for mixing
Blank paper for practising

---

### ♦ twisted ribbon ♦

Squeeze small portions of Gold and Raw Umber on to the lid and fill the base of the container with water. Mix a little of the colours together with the brush, wipe it on the edge of the lid, then dip it into the Raw Umber and, turning the brush over, dip the other side into the Gold. Do not overload the brush. Make a brush stroke by pressing down on the paper, then releasing the pressure and twisting the point of the brush at the same time. Press–release–twist: these movements combined will give the twisted and shaded effect

### ♦ for an uneven wired ribbon ♦

Sketch faintly first with chalk and paint in sections using the same method as for twisted ribbon, but returning to strengthen the shading

### ♦ bows ♦

Use the same ribbon technique for the bow which is tackled in separate sections (see diagram). The two shades of paint on the brush combined with 'press–release–twist' are the basic steps to follow. It is a good idea to draw a bow onto the surface of the work in chalk which can be removed when the bow is dry. It will take a little practice but, like riding a bike, once you get the hang of it you will never forget!

### ♦ leaves ♦

Over the centuries leaves have been used to decorate furniture and are painted in many different forms. The following are simple ways to decorate and enhance your work. A No. 2 or 3 brush is best. Until you are confident it may be helpful to draw a straight line faintly first in chalk. Using the two-colour technique (dark colour one side of the brush and the paler (or white or gold) on the other), place the side tip of the brush on to the surface with a little pressure, make a small stroke using the tip of the brush in a slight flicking movement which will form the point of the leaf, releasing all pressure as you do so. Draw a short straight stem-line with the tip of the brush and carry on into the leaf, add another beneath it and so on

### ♦ curling stems ♦

Paint a thin curving line first. Add short stems and leaves on either side in the same way as before

### ♦ berries ♦

Dip the tip of the brush into neat paint in the darkest colour and stipple on to the surface using the end tip of the brush only; follow this by dipping the brush into white, again without water, and repeat

*COMBINE TWISTED RIBBON with curling stems and berries to create a pretty border design*

TWISTED RIBBONS

UNEVEN WIRED RIBBONS

BOWS

LEAVES

CURLING STEMS

BERRIES

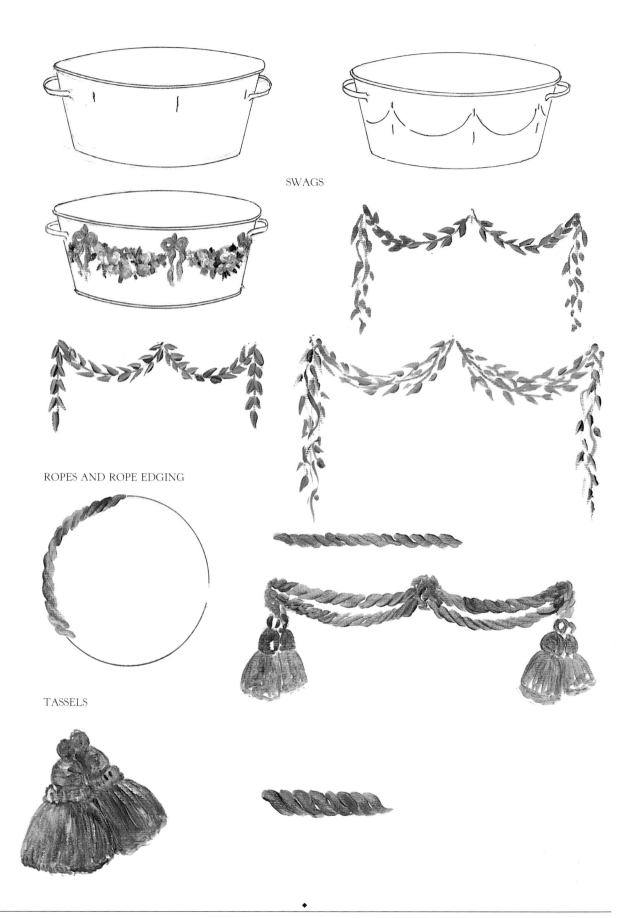

SWAGS

ROPES AND ROPE EDGING

TASSELS

### ◆ *swags* ◆

Swags, ribbons and roses are my favourite theme! Quick and simple to paint, you will soon find they present no difficulty. Make three equidistant chalk marks and join them together with curved lines, shallow or deep, in the shape of a swag. Apply the découpage design, roughly following the curved lines. When the design is complete, dry and cleaned up, the lines can be redrawn as a guide. Paint swags of bows and ribbons, leaves or ropes. Leaves can be painted either from the centre outwards or to meet in the middle

### ◆ *tassels* ◆

Mark out in chalk first then sketch the tassels in thinned-down paint to mark out their shape exactly. Fill in with the deepest colour (raw umber in this case) shading the strands with gold until they look realistic. Highlight with white

### ◆ *ropes and rope edging* ◆

The shape of the brush stroke is a shallow 'S' laid down at an angle

## *Ageing and antiquing with craquelure*

### ◆ *materials list* ◆

**CRACKLE VARNISH**
Two-bottle pack available from artists' suppliers
2.5cm (1 inch) brush
Tube of Raw Umber artists' oil paint
White spirit  ◆  Old tablespoon
Kitchen paper
Semi-matt varnish, polyurethane lacquer or pale
  eggshell varnish
Beeswax, gedgewax or white wax (for polishing
  furniture when it is completely finished and
  dry)
Soft cloth
Hairdrier and long extension cord

Almost all old furniture and some antiques which have been newly painted can be enhanced by a subtle craquelure finish. Reproduction furniture is often greatly improved by first painting and then adding an antiqued craquelure finish, but such pieces need to have the right 'bone structure' and look convincing when finished.

Crackle varnish is sold as a pack containing two bottles of varnish which interact to produce cracks. The first to be applied is a dark slow-drying ageing varnish and the second is a very brittle fast-drying water-based varnish. As the water-based brittle crackling varnish dries rapidly it interacts with the slow-drying flexible ageing varnish and splits into hairline cracks. The process is unpredictable and the skill lies in knowing exactly when to apply the second varnish. The first

*TABLETOP with an antique craquelure finish*

should feel slightly tacky, 'dry-tacky' and not sticky before brushing on the crackling varnish.

### • applying a craquelure finish •

1 If the piece is decorated with découpage, apply a single protective coat of semi-matt varnish and leave to dry before applying the first craquelure varnish. If the piece is undecorated, the first craquelure varnish may be applied direct to the painted surface.

2 The first varnish should be applied thinly and evenly, brushing it out smoothly over the surface. When it is 'dry-tacky' to the touch, brush on a more generous coat of the fast-drying water-based 'crackle' varnish. Ensure the first varnish is covered entirely otherwise you will be left with dirty looking sticky patches! Leave to dry for approximately 60 minutes. If no cracks appear a little encouragement is required by heating the surface with a hairdrier. The surface should be covered with delicate hair-line cracks which are almost imperceptible. It should *not* look like clay which has cracked open in the sun!

3 The next stage is to apply the antique finish. Mix white spirit with Raw Umber artists' oil tube colour – usually about 2.5cm (1 inch) of Raw Umber to about 2 or 3 tablespoons of white spirit. Mash the oil colour with a little of the white spirit until smooth with no lumps,

then pour into the container adding more white spirit. (The consistency can be anywhere between cold coffee and double cream.) Paint on; then, after 10 or 15 minutes, wipe off the decoration first with kitchen paper, leaving the antiquing fluid in logical places where dust would normally collect. Renew the kitchen paper frequently, 'polishing' the surface until the paper looks almost clean, pushing the colour into the cracks. Leave to dry overnight.

4 *The next day* apply a coat of semi-matt varnish, polyurethane lacquer, or pale eggshell varnish. Let it dry thoroughly. Paint with a second coat of varnish and leave to dry for a day or two.

*NOTE* As the top coat of the craquelure finish is water based, the application of varnish is essential. For a satin-like patina, rub on a generous amount of natural beeswax polish, Mylands gedge wax or white wax and leave to dry for about 15 minutes. Take a soft cloth and buff up in the direction of the grain. The surface will look wonderful and can be waxed several times and treated as any fine piece of furniture.

The foregoing method of antiquing is probably the most common, but there are other antiquing compounds which can be applied to painted furniture, etc and which you might like to try:

• Scumble glaze may be used by mixing artists' oil paint and transparent oil glaze 1:8, adding the glaze slowly to the paint. (Light colours are not suitable for tinting an oil glaze as they will yellow in a matter of months)

• Emulsion paint and/or artists' acrylics mixed with water to make a brown wash

• Brown wax polish

• White wax polish mixed with rottenstone and fuller's earth powder
(*NOTE* Do not apply varnish to this surface)

• Brown boot polish

• Cold coffee

Colours used for antiquing are usually the earth colours Raw Umber, Burnt Umber, Raw Sienna, Payne's Grey and Terra Verde.

### • paint categories •

All paint is either water-based, oil-based or spirit-based. It is not possible to mix oil-based and water-based paints. Water-based paints such as emulsion will not easily adhere to a surface covered with an oil-based paint. Sometimes adding a few drops of washing-up liquid may help, but it is more usual to create a barrier between the two by applying a coat of shellac varnish which is spirit-based.

**Oil-based products include:**
Oil primers including aluminium and red oxide
Oil undercoats
Satinwood paint
Eggshell finishes
Gloss finishes
Scumble glaze (transparent oil glaze)
Enamels
Polyurethane lacquers
Craquelure first coat (the ageing varnish – see page 25)
Wax polishes and liming wax.

Dilute products and clean brushes with white spirit; wash brushes in soap and water afterwards.

**Water-based products include:**
Acrylic primer undercoat
Vinyl matt emulsion paint (known as flat latex in the USA)
Vinyl silk emulsion paint (latex eggshell in the USA)
Vinyl satin emulsion paint
Emulsion glaze
Unibond/PVA adhesive (used in emulsion glaze)
Acrylic tubepaints
PVA paints
Acrylic mediums and varnishes
Craquelure second coat (see page 25).

Dilute paint with water; clean brushes thoroughly in soap and water.

**Spirit-based products include:**
Car spray paints
Cellulose-based enamels
Hammerite
Shellac varnish
Cellulose lacquer
Spirit stainers.

The solvent for shellac and all the spirit-based paints is methylated spirit. Dilute shellac varnish with a small amount of solvent before use, and keep a small amount in a glass jar (plastic containers will disintegrate) to stand your brush in to keep it soft – remember it evaporates.

## SOLVING DÉCOUPAGE PROBLEMS

Here are some of the more common problems you may encounter – and their solutions.

•   *TEARS* or surface damage to the paper cutouts when pasted. The paper, weakened by the wet paste may occasionally tear when you are pressing out air bubbles and excess glue. It is usually impossible to butt the two pieces without the tear being obvious, so you must do one of the following:
(a) remove the cutout immediately with craft knife and cut out another;
(b) if it is stuck down and drying, cut an identical piece and stick it over the damaged one;
(c) if the tear is small, overlay another cutout over the damaged part: slap a butterfly on it, for instance;
(d) as a last resort soak off the cutout with water on a bristle art brush, working the brush behind it until it leaves the surface. Dry the piece off and start again!
•   *TO MINIMIZE TEARS*, always let the decoration dry out before attempting to clean the surface up with a damp (not wet) sponge.
•   *RUNS IN THE VARNISH*, especially where the varnish has collected around the base of a handle or under a rim and run or dribbled and dried. With a sharp craft knife blade carefully pare it off – don't dig the blade in deeply otherwise you will go back to the base surface. Once removed, sand gently with 240 grade sandpaper or flourpaper, remove dust with a takcloth and revarnish.
•   *GOLD SPREADS OVER THE SURFACE* of the work with the first brush stroke when applying the varnish. There is nothing you can do to cure the problem, but to avoid it in the first place by using water-based acrylic gold underneath varnish. Apply a suitable finish such as Humbrol liquid leaf, enamel gold, treasure wax, etc after the varnishing stage.

# 2
# STYLISH ACCESSORIES
# FOR THE KITCHEN

*W*hether your kitchen is a warm hub of life and activity where the family congregate for meals or a small, efficient and labour-saving one, some items are found almost universally: a tray, breadbin, a set of canisters. Why not decorate something to brighten up your kitchen and provide an attractive focal point?

◆ ◆ ◆ ◆ ◆

# ROUND BREADBIN

*Add a little style to your kitchen! Smarten up a plain enamel breadbin by painting and designing it to match your colour scheme and it will certainly be a talking point among your family and friends. Darkest green or terracotta are particularly suitable background colours for a country home but black or navy blue and dark rich red look more sophisticated in a town or city. You will enjoy using large flowers which make a wonderful splash of colour on any dark background.*

---

### ◆ materials list ◆

**ROUND BREADBIN**
**PREPARATION**
Red oxide metal primer
An old 2.5cm (1 inch) brush
White spirit
Kitchen paper
**PAINTING**
250ml tin of vinyl matt emulsion paint in a dark
    country green (or colour of your choice)
    2.5cm (1 inch) brush
**DÉCOUPAGE**
Good-quality wrapping paper of your choice
Small sharp scissors
Craft knife
Wallpaper adhesive
Glue brush
Pasting board
Small sponge or kitchen paper
Piece of white chalk
**ANTIQUE GOLD**
Small tubes of Gold and Raw Umber artists'
    acrylics
No. 4 or 5 artist's brush
Lidded container or jar
Water to mix
**VARNISHING**
Takcloth
Small tin of semi-matt pale craft varnish
2.5cm (1 inch) brush

---

### ◆ preparation ◆

*1* Prepare the breadbin as instructed on pages 15–18. If the breadbin is to be functional, do not paint the inner surfaces with red oxide primer.

◄ *LARGE FLOWERS brighten up an old breadbin*

*2* When the red oxide metal primer is completely dry, apply the dark green paint. (No undercoat is necessary as a dark topcoat is being used.) There is no need to wait for long between applications as water-based paint dries very quickly. Apply three or four coats until you achieve a perfect finish. Allow to dry completely.

### ◆ découpage ◆

*1* Cut out a wide selection of flowers and leaves, etc. There are many possible designs and with a little practice you will find out what pleases you best. Some of the cutouts could be formed into the beginnings of a design on a surface beside you, or you could stick on a couple of pieces and build up the design as you go along. It is sometimes easier to turn the bin on its side in your lap and place several shapes on it to see if you like the effect. Chalk carefully around the edge of the motifs leaving their outline on the bin. This gives a good guide when you stand the bin upright again and begin pasting and attaching the pieces to the surface.
*2* Turn each paper cutout singly face down on to the pasting board and paste the glue evenly over the surface, making sure the edges are covered. Turn right side up using a craft knife and apply to the surface of the bin, using the chalk marks for guidance. Work out the air bubbles and excess glue with a rolling finger movement, wiping the glue away with kitchen paper. When the surface is flat press the edges down. If desired, apply small motifs to the lid also. Leave to dry out.
*3* Clean up the work with a small damp sponge working from the centre of the motifs out toward the edges to remove the glue from both the decoration and the background.

### ◆ finishing ◆

Apply an antique gold finish to the rim of the bin as described on page 13. Leave to dry, then varnish as described on pages 13–14.

*BLOSSOM BREADBIN Here is another idea for decorating a breadbin, a simple white blossom design which is reproduced from a gorgeous Dutch masters painting published by National Gallery Publications Ltd. This paper requires careful cutting to remove the background but fortunately it is black too! Follow the step-by-step instructions on page 29, changing the colour of the paint to suit*

*DECORATED WITH an easy-to-cut motif, these canisters will cheer up any kitchen*

# A Collection of Canisters

*Canisters are plentiful in junk shops and at flea markets; perhaps you have a set at home. They come in various shapes and sizes but do check that the lids belong to the bases as they are frequently a marriage and ill-fitting. The set of canisters in the photograph is painted in a dark country green and decorated in a bright and cheerful primula design which is very simple to cut and quick to do.*

## ◆ materials list ◆

**CANISTERS OF VARIOUS SIZES**

**PREPARATION**
Red oxide metal primer
An old 2.5cm (1 inch) brush
White spirit
Kitchen paper

**PAINTING**
250ml tin of vinyl matt emulsion paint in dark
  green
2.5cm (1 inch) brush

**DÉCOUPAGE**
Wrapping paper
Small sharp scissors
Craft knife
Wallpaper adhesive
Glue brush
Pasting board
Small sponge or kitchen paper

**ANTIQUE GOLD**
Small tubes of Gold and Raw Umber artists'
  acrylics
No. 4 artist's brush
Lidded container or jar
Water to mix

**VARNISHING**
Takcloth
Small tin of semi-matt varnish or polyurethane
  lacquer
2.5cm (1 inch) brush

## ◆ preparation ◆

1   Prepare the tinware as described on pages 15–18. If the canisters are to be used for storing food, do not paint the inner surfaces with red oxide primer.

2   When the red oxide is dry apply two coats of dark green emulsion to the outer surface of each canister, letting it dry after each coat. Turn the canisters upside down and paint the bases.

## ◆ découpage ◆

1   Cut out blocks of flowers and leaves and apply in a random fashion around the base of each canister. Fill in with single flowers and leaves wherever necessary.

2   Turn each cutout singly face down on to the pasting board and apply the glue evenly making sure the edges are covered. Turn right side up using a craft knife and apply to the surface, working out any air bubbles and excess glue with your fingers and wiping off with kitchen paper. When the surface is flat, press down the edges. Leave to dry.

3   Decorate the lids and leave them to dry.

4   Clean up the work and background paint with a damp sponge, working from the centre of the design out towards the edges. Leave to dry.

## ◆ finishing ◆

Apply an antique gold finish to the canister rims as described on page 13. Leave to dry, then varnish as described on pages 13–14.

# FAT COFFEE POT

*The squat, sturdy shape of this old coffee pot attracted me to buy it. The lovely paper includes antique roses and lilies in its design and is one that I have used several times in the book. I think it is ideal for the coffee pot.*

### • materials list •

**COFFEE POT**
**PREPARATION**
Red oxide metal primer
An old 2.5cm (1 inch) brush
White spirit
Kitchen paper
**PAINTING**
Small tin of white acrylic primer undercoat
Small tin vinyl silk emulsion paint in cream
2.5cm (1 inch) brush
**DÉCOUPAGE**
Wrapping paper with large blooms
Small sharp scissors
Craft knife
Wallpaper adhesive
Glue brush
Pasting board
Small sponge or kitchen paper
**ANTIQUE GOLD**
Small tubes of Gold and Raw Umber artists'
    acrylics
No. 4 artist's brush
Lidded container or jar
Water to mix
**VARNISHING**
Takcloth
Small tin of semi-matt varnish or polyurethane
    lacquer
2.5cm (1 inch) brush

### • preparation •

1   Prepare the pot as described on pages 15–18. If the pot is to be functional, do not apply red oxide primer to the inner surface.
2   When the red oxide is completely dry, apply at least two coats of white acrylic primer undercoat until the surface is well covered, allowing to dry between coats. Turn the pot upside down and paint the base.
3   Overcoat the pot with vinyl silk – two or three coats will probably be required – and let it dry.

### • découpage •

1   Select a few beautiful blooms and cut them out meticulously: any mistakes will be very noticeable on the pale background. Choose a few flowers with long curling

stems to stick at the base of the handle to bring the designs on the two sides together. A fairly delicate and curving bloom or bud with a twisting stem would enhance the decoration on the lid.

2   Turn each cutout singly face down on to the pasting board and spread the glue evenly over the surface, ensuring the edges are covered. Turn right side up using a craft knife and stick on to the pot, working out air bubbles and excess glue with your fingertips. Leave to dry.

3   Using a small damp sponge and working from the centre of the design out towards the edges, clean the excess glue from both the decoration and the background.

### ✦ *finishing* ✦

Apply an antique gold finish to the rim and handle of the coffee pot as described on page 13. Leave to dry, then varnish as described on pages 13–14.

✦

# 3
# *TRANSFORMING EVERYDAY ITEMS*

*M*ost of us have things we use almost without noticing how shabby they have become; a tea-caddy, biscuit tin or cake tin perhaps, an old tray, boxes in numerous shapes and sizes tucked away in a cupboard or at the back of a drawer. Let them see the light of day, give them a coat of paint, cut a pretty design and they will become both useful and decorative. In this chapter there are several such items; you may have other things at home which would benefit from a facelift and I hope the following ideas will inspire you.

♦ ♦ ♦ ♦

# RED TIN WITH ROSES

*An unusually shaped tin which once held biscuits or chocolates, a rusty black tin deedbox, any old tin box in fact. All can be given a new lease of life becoming, after a complete facelift, much admired objects of beauty.*

## • materials list •

**AN OLD TIN BOX**

**PREPARATION**
Red oxide metal primer
An old 2.5cm (1 inch) brush
White spirit  •  Kitchen paper

**PAINTING**
250ml tin of dark red vinyl matt or smallest
    vinyl silk emulsion
2.5cm (1 inch) brush

**DÉCOUPAGE**
8 lovely full blown roses, leaves and stems cut
    from 3 sheets of paper
Small sharp scissors  •  Craft knife
Wallpaper adhesive  •  Glue brush
Pasting board
Small sponge or kitchen paper
Piece of white chalk

**ANTIQUE GOLD**
Small tubes of Gold and Raw Umber artists'
    acrylics
No. 4 artist's brush
Lidded container or jar  •  Water to mix

**VARNISHING**
Takcloth  •  Small tin of semi-matt varnish
2.5cm (1 inch) brush

**FINAL TOUCHES**
Suitably sized piece of self-adhesive suede
    velvet
Kitchen scissors

## • preparation •

1  Prepare the box as described on pages 15–18.
2  When the red oxide metal primer is completely dry, apply at least four coats of the dark red paint. This may look pale red or even pink in the tin, but the colour will intensify and darken as more coats are applied. Allow each coat to dry before applying the next.

◀ *A RUSTY DEEDBOX is given a new lease of life*

## • découpage •

1  Cut out approximately 8 roses with stems and leaves. Take care to cut around the thorns – well worth the effort as they look marvellous against the background.
2  Arrange the flowers and leaves in a circular or oval shape, overlapping slightly. When you are happy with the design, hold it down with the flat of your hand and, with a piece of white chalk, draw around the design to leave an outline. This will be a useful guide when you are pasting and trying to remember where each piece was in your original design!
3  Turn each paper cutout singly face down on to the pasting board. Apply the glue evenly over the surface making sure the edges are covered, pasting over the fine stems on to the board. A craft knife will be helpful for lifting them.
4  Turn the cutouts right side up using a craft knife and line up with the chalk marks on the box, gently straightening out each flower and stem until it is flat (fine stems can crease). Work out the air bubbles and excess glue with a rolling finger movement, wiping away glue with kitchen paper and pressing down the edges when the cutout is flat. When complete, leave to dry.
5  Clean up the surface of the design and background carefully with damp kitchen paper or a small sponge. Leave to dry.

## • finishing •

Apply an antique gold finish to the rim of the box as described on page 13. Leave to dry, then varnish as described on pages 13–14. Apply the first coat of varnish sparingly to avoid the wonderful white roses absorbing the varnish and becoming discoloured. Leave to dry for a day or two.

## • final touches •

Place the base of the box on to the paper backing of the self-adhesive suede velvet and draw round it to mark out the shape. Cut along the marked lines, peel off the backing and stick the velvet to the base of the box to protect your furniture and provide a professional finish.

# FLOWERED TRAY

*This old tray had been kicking around the house for years. Its composition is unknown but no matter, it was paintable and ripe for transformation. This project uses a simple sponged-on paint-finish to create an interesting background.*

## • materials list •

**ANY NON-METALLIC TRAY**
**PREPARATION**
Fine grade sandpaper/glasspaper
**PAINTING**
Small tin of white acrylic primer undercoat
Small tin of white vinyl silk emulsion
2.5cm (1 inch) brush
Small tin of Unibond/PVA
Trial-size pot of cream vinyl matt or vinyl silk
    emulsion
Small natural sea-sponge
Container for mixing glaze
Water to mix
**DÉCOUPAGE**
Wrapping paper with an abundance of flower
    heads
Small sharp scissors
Craft knife
Wallpaper adhesive
Small glue brush
Pasting board
Small sponge or kitchen paper
**ANTIQUE GOLD**
Small tubes of Gold and Raw Umber artists'
    acrylics
No. 4 artist's brush
Lidded container or jar
Water to mix
**VARNISHING**
Takcloth
Small tin of semi-matt pale craft varnish
2.5cm (1 inch) brush
Fine-grade sandpaper

## • preparation •

*1*  Apply two or three coats of acrylic primer undercoat allowing to dry between coats. (Acrylic paint is fast drying as it is water based.)
*2*  Paint with two coats of white vinyl silk emulsion.
*3*  Mix an emulsion glaze by combining one tablespoon of Unibond/PVA adhesive with one tablespoon of cream matt or silk emulsion and two or three tablespoons of water.
*4*  Dip the tip of the damp sea-sponge into the glaze and squeeze out. With a light movement dab the sponge over the surface of the tray, moving the sponge in different directions to avoid a regimented design. This should take no more than 30 minutes to dry.

## • découpage •

*1*  Cut a good number of flower heads and a few leaves. Lay on the edge of the tray in a line or in small groups.
*2*  Set out pasting board, wallpaper paste, glue brush, small sponge and a container of water. Paste each flower head separately and apply to the tray. A craft knife will be helpful to lift small pasted cutouts from the board. Continue until the design around the edge is finished.
*3*  A second line of flower heads may be applied. My tray originally appeared rather bare but when another line of flower heads was added in a scalloped shape the tray took on a much more cheerful appearance. A small posy of flowers decorates the centre of the tray.
*4*  When the pasted on design is dry, clean off the excess glue from the flowers and the background with a damp sponge working outwards from the centre of the blooms taking care not to scuff the edges. Allow to dry.

## • finishing •

Apply an antique gold finish around the tray as described on page 13. Allow to dry, then varnish as described on pages 13–14. If the tray is to be functional it will require at least 10 coats of varnish, but you could get away with fewer if it is for decorative purposes only.

*EASY TO CUT and stick, pansies over a simple sponged paint-finish beautify an old tray. The object to the top right of the tray, similarly decorated, is an Edwardian bedpan!*

# EDWARDIAN ENAMEL JUG

*This beautiful old Edwardian jug was found quite fortuitously. It was discoloured, dirty and green with algae when it was spotted in a friend's greenhouse where it had been used for watering the plants. Needless to say it was rescued immediately – with stunning results.*

*The jug was painted in Dulux Gardenia, and simply splodged all over very lightly with a sponge dipped in a soft ochre emulsion glaze. This is a speedy way of achieving a broken paint-finish.*

THESE EXQUISITE LILIES
with deep blue convolvulus
blend beautifully with the
sponged background to create
a delicate and yet rather
sophisticated effect which
would fit into almost any
setting. The paper is by
Caspari.
Photographed on an
embroidered silk antique
shawl against a little hand-
painted Victorian mirror and
filled with sweet-smelling
stargazer lilies, it is
accompanied by one of my
favourite birthday gifts, a
heavily gilded Minton
compote holding fragile white
roses gathered from a friend's
garden to complete the light
theme

## • *materials list* •

**ENAMEL JUG**

**PREPARATION**
Red oxide metal primer
An old 2.5cm (1 inch) brush
White spirit
Kitchen roll

**PAINTING**
Small tin of white acrylic primer undercoat
Small tin of Gardenia vinyl silk emulsion
2.5cm (1 inch) brush
Small Unibond/PVA adhesive
Small white acrylic matt or vinyl silk emulsion
Small amount of Yellow Ochre artists' acrylic
    tube paint
Small natural sponge
Lidded container or jar
Water to mix

**DÉCOUPAGE**
Wrapping paper
Small sharp scissors
Craft knife
Wallpaper adhesive
Glue brush
Pasting board
Small sponge or kitchen paper

**ANTIQUE GOLD**
Small tubes of Gold and Raw Umber artists'
    acrylics
No. 4 artist's brush
Lidded container or jar
Water to mix

**VARNISHING**
Takcloth
Small tin of semi-matt varnish
2.5cm (1 inch) brush

## • *preparation* •

1  Prepare the jug as described on pages 15–18.
2  When the red oxide metal primer is dry, apply two or three coats of acrylic primer undercoat allowing it to dry between coats.
3  Apply two or three coats of Gardenia vinyl silk until the surface looks perfect, allow to dry between coats.
4  Prepare an emulsion glaze by combining one tablespoon of Unibond/PVA adhesive, one tablespoon of white acrylic vinyl matt (or silk) emulsion, a small squeeze of Yellow Ochre artists' acrylic and three tablespoons water to mix. Squeeze the sponge out in clean water and dab on to kitchen roll to remove excess moisture. Dip part of the sponge into the ochre emulsion glaze and lightly sponge over the surface of the jug using a random motion. Leave to dry.

## • *découpage* •

1  Cut out the lilies and convolvulus taking care with the fine curling stems. If you find them difficult to handle, cut them into sections and butt them together when they are pasted on to the surface.
2  Place each cutout singly face down on to the pasting board and brush on the glue evenly over the surface ensuring the edges are covered. Turn right side up – the craft knife will be useful for this and for lifting the curling stems into position – and place on the surface of the jug.
*NOTE*  it is tricky to stick large paper cutouts absolutely flat as the surface is bulbous and they tend to crease. When they are wet with paste they do stretch slightly with care as you are pressing out the glue, or a small incision may be made on the outer edge of a flower to avoid creasing. Leave to dry.
3  Clean off the excess glue from the work using a small damp sponge or kitchen paper.

## • *finishing* •

Apply an antique gold finish to the rim of the jug as described on page 13. Leave to dry, then varnish as described on pages 13–14, taking care that the varnish does not run from the handle or the top rim.

# DECORATIVE BOX

*Most of us have one or two old boxes tucked away in a cupboard or relegated to the back of a drawer. The box in the picture was a fifties jewellery box which had been covered in thin leather and lined in jap silk. The leather took time to soak off but afterwards the pine box rubbed down easily. The paint effect was done with a fan brush and the cords and tassels hand-painted. Odd pieces of fabric have been used to line the box so that it can revert to its original function or double up as a small sewing box.*

*ROPES AND TASSELS on a fan finish adorn this beautiful box*

◆

## • materials list •

**WOODEN BOX WITH HINGED LID**
**PREPARATION**
100 grade and 240 grade sandpaper/glasspaper
**PAINTING**
Small tin of white acrylic primer
2.5cm (1 inch) or smaller brush
250ml tin of Terracotta vinyl matt emulsion or
    another colour of your choice
250ml tin of white vinyl matt emulsion or a small
    tube of Chinese White artists' acrylic tube
    paint   •   No. 6 fan brush
Lidded container
**CAMEO**
Piece of white chalk
Sample pot of Gardenia or pale ivory emulsion
Small brush to apply – a cheap soft glue brush
    would fit the bill
**DÉCOUPAGE**
Good quality wrapping paper or a picture taken
    from a gardening or horticultural diary or
    botanical print
Small sharp scissors   •   Craft knife
Wallpaper adhesive
Glue brush   •   Pasting board
Small sponge or kitchen paper
**HAND-PAINTED DECORATION**
Small tubes of Gold and Raw Umber artists' acrylics
White paint as listed above
No. 4 artist's brush
Lidded container   •   Water to mix
**VARNISHING**
Takcloth
Small tin of semi-matt varnish or polyurethane
    lacquer
2.5cm (1 inch) brush   •   White spirit
**FINAL TOUCHES**
Suitably sized piece of self-adhesive suede velvet
    fabric or wallpaper to line interior

## • preparation •

*1*  Repair (if necessary) and sand your box.
*2*  Remove dust and dirt from the inside and out, then apply a coat of acrylic primer undercoat. Let it dry before applying the second and third coats.
*3*  Apply two coats of Terracotta vinyl matt emulsion (or colour of your choice) and let it dry. Take the fan brush and dip one side of it into white paint, the other

into the Terracotta. Pull it towards you, wiggling it in any direction, replenishing either or both colours as you work (see page 21). Cover the entire surface with the pattern, propping up the lid to avoid sticking. Leave to dry.

## • the cameo •

Draw the oval shape of the cameo on top of the paint-finish with white chalk (it can be dusted off to make alterations). With a small brush apply two or three coats of white undercoat letting it dry between coats. Once the cameo looks solid white, apply the ivory or Gardenia paint – two coats should be sufficient.

## • découpage •

*1*  Choose a few beautiful blooms and arrange within the cameo.
*2*  When the design looks balanced stick the underneath pieces first. Turn each paper cutout singly face down on the pasting board and brush the glue evenly over the surface ensuring the edges are covered. Place the cutout into position, press air bubbles and excess glue out to the edges and wipe with kitchen paper. When the flowers are flat, press the edges down. Leave to dry.
*3*  Using a small piece of damp sponge or kitchen paper, remove excess glue from the background paint and from the design. Leave to dry.

## • ropes and tassels decoration •

*1*  Using a No. 4 artist's brush mix a small portion of Raw Umber and Gold together mixing it rather dark to start. Paint a rope around the cameo (see page 25) and let it dry. Go over it a second time highlighting logical areas.
*2*  Make small chalk marks to indicate the centre of the front, back and sides and continue with the rope design. Don't worry if your line isn't absolutely true, it can become a double cord to balance things out as mine has!
*3*  Finally, draw the tassels (page 25) with a pale mix of white and Raw Umber; fill in with deeper umber and gold until the tassels look realistic and highlight with white. Decorate the box's keyhole if there is one.

## • finishing •

When the work is dry, remove dust and apply a coat of varnish to the oval cameo. Subsequent coats should cover the entire box. Prop the lid open to avoid sticking. Cover the base of the box with self-adhesive suede velvet, and line with fabric or wallpaper.

# CHRISTMAS PLATTERS AND PLATES

*Unusually shaped platters or sizeable plates are devilish difficult to find unless they are of porcelain or pottery. Purely functional new enamelware is available from hardware stores, and you might be able to find a selection of unusual items in white enamel which could be decorated, failing that use old crockery plates. During the Christmas holiday one never seems to have enough plates in the house to use for sweetmeats, nuts, etc and these will be a welcome addition. Remind willing helpers after the party that they must not be immersed in water!*

## ◆ materials list ◆

**PREPARATION – ENAMEL PLATTERS AND PLATES**

Small tin of red oxide metal primer

An old 2.5cm (1 inch) brush

White spirit ◆ Kitchen paper

**PREPARATION – POTTERY PLATES**

An emulsion glaze mixing 1 tablespoon of
    Unibond with one of white emulsion to 2 parts
    water. Apply two coats and allow to dry
    thoroughly before painting on a colour.

2.5cm (1 inch) brush or smaller

**PAINTING**

250ml tin vinyl matt emulsion paint in a dark
    joyful colour

**DÉCOUPAGE**

Hand-painted Christmas paper illustrated with
    holly, ivy, mistletoe or other Christmastime
    flora

Small sharp scissors

Craft knife

Wallpaper adhesive

Glue brush

Pasting board

Small sponge or kitchen paper

**ANTIQUE GOLD**

Small tubes of Gold and Raw Umber artists'
    acrylics

No. 4 artist's brush

Lidded container or jar

Water to mix

**VARNISHING**

Takcloth

Small tin of semi-matt varnish or polyurethane
    lacquer

2.5cm (1 inch) brush ◆ White spirit

## ◆ preparation ◆

1  Prepare enamel plate(s) as described on pages 15–18.

2  When the oxide or emulsion glaze is dry apply two or three coats of your chosen colour, brushing the paint on in one direction for a neat finish and allowing it to dry between coats.

## ◆ découpage ◆

1  Carefully cut one or two attractive sprays or blooms and leaves for each plate.

2  Turn each cutout singly face down on to the pasting board and brush the glue evenly over the surface ensuring that the edges are covered. Using a craft knife, turn right side up and position on the plate, working out any excess glue and air bubbles with a rolling movement of the fingers. When the cutout is flat press down the edges and wipe away the glue with damp kitchen roll.

3  When the design is finished, leave it to dry completely before cleaning up the surface with a damp sponge or kitchen paper to remove any dried glue.

## ◆ finishing ◆

Apply an antique gold finish to the outer edge of the plate as described on page 13 or decorate it with leaves (see page 22). Leave to dry, then varnish as described on pages 13–14.

▶ *CHRISTMAS PLATTERS have been decorated with paper hand-painted by Sandra Wall-Armitage. It was tricky to dissect the mistletoe and holly from the ivy, but well worth the effort*

# 4
# SPRINGTIME

Snowdrops, hellebores and crocuses provide early colour in the garden; now with the first warm days and birdsong in the air, wild primroses cover the high banks along the lanes and deep purple violets and wood aconites are showing their tiny faces.

A most inspiring paper which has been skilfully hand-painted by Sandra Wall-Armitage depicts violets which are so realistic one can almost feel their fragility and smell their delicate fragrance, a variegated ivy, crocuses, buttercups and snowdrops – the first breath of spring!

One sheet goes a long way as it is possible to dissect each species separately. The crocuses on the paper appear lifelike but this quality tends to be diminished when they are cut out unless treated with imagination. As they are so straight they can be tucked under one another in the design to give movement and life.

◆ ◆ ◆ ◆

# BOTTLE COASTERS

*Primrose yellow and leaf-green paint are a perfect foil for the spring flowers on the design. Simple paint-finished backgrounds add more interest if you feel like experimenting. A pair of pretty coasters would be a unique and individual gift and a most acceptable wedding present for a spring bride, especially if they were accompanied by two bottles of fine champagne!*

▶ *TINY GALLERIED TRAYS The coasters and trays use different flowers cut from the same paper. The two trays have been decorated with spring flowers applied to a primrose yellow background in exactly the same way as the coasters. The violets require accurate cutting and careful pasting. The stems of the crocuses have been tucked under the ivy to avoid looking too straight; this is achieved by sticking down the crocuses first and placing the ivy leaves slightly overlapping the crocus stems, a technique known as overlaying. Leave work to dry out before attempting to clean off any excess glue from the background and the paper decoration. Care should be taken when varnishing as the varnish is apt to collect around the edge of the tray where the base meets the sides. Brush the varnish on the inner sides first before varnishing the base of the tray. Varnish the outside edge of the tray until it is the same colour*

◆

## • materials list •

**TWO OR MORE BOTTLE COASTERS**

**PREPARATION**

100 grade sandpaper

**PAINTING**

Small tin of acrylic primer undercoat

2.5cm (1 inch) brush

Sample pot or 250ml tin of primrose yellow
  emulsion **or** small tin white vinyl silk
  emulsion (if a paint-finish is to be applied)

Materials for paint-finish if required (see
  page 19)

**DÉCOUPAGE**

Wrapping paper by Sandra Wall-Armitage
  illustrated with spring flowers

Small sharp scissors   •   Craft knife

Wallpaper adhesive   •   Glue brush

Pasting board

Small sponge or kitchen paper

**ANTIQUE GOLD**

Small tubes of Gold and Raw Umber artists'
  acrylics

No. 4 or 5 artist's brush

Lidded container or jar   •   Water to mix

**VARNISHING**

Takcloth

Small tin of semi-matt varnish or polyurethane
  lacquer

2.5cm (1 inch) brush

Fine-grade sandpaper   •   White spirit

**FINAL TOUCHES**

Small piece of soft green self-adhesive suede
  velvet

Kitchen scissors

## • preparation •

*1*  Rub the edges and surface of the coaster(s) with 100 grade sandpaper. Remove dust, apply first coat of undercoat and let it dry. Sand the coaster(s) again until smooth. Remove dust and paint on a second coat. Leave to dry.
*2*  Paint the coaster with two coats of yellow emulsion letting it dry between coats.

## • optional paint-finishes •

Prepare as above, using a white vinyl silk topcoat instead of yellow. Then apply either a yellow or three-colour sponged finish as described below.

**Yellow sponged finish** Mix an emulsion glaze using one tablespoon of yellow emulsion, one tablespoon of Unibond/PVA and two or three tablespoons of water. Using the tip of a sea-sponge, sponge on the glaze with light, dabbing movements over the entire surface and let it dry.

**Three-colour sponging** Mix an emulsion glaze using one tablespoon of the white vinyl silk emulsion used for the topcoat, one tablespoon of Unibond/PVA and two or three tablespoons of water.

Using the lid as a palette, squeeze out small amounts of Yellow Ochre, Acid Yellow and Chinese White artists' acrylics (or emulsion paints of those colours – measure with a spoon if using emulsion). Dip the sponge in the glaze first before touching one or more of the colours with the tip. Sponge on diagonally, building up the colour gradually. Let it dry. The inside of the coaster(s) may be painted in a contrasting colour, for example leaf-green.

## • découpage •

*1*  Choose your favourite spring flowers and cut them into tiny sprigs and flower heads. Turn each paper cutout singly face down on the pasting board and brush the glue evenly over the surface ensuring the edges are covered. Place the cutout into position, press air bubbles and excess glue out to the edges and wipe away with kitchen paper. When the flowers are flat, press the edges down. A craft knife is useful for lifting small cutouts. Apply to each facet of the coaster and allow to dry thoroughly.
*2*  Choose a pretty central motif for the inside of the coaster. Apply as above and allow to dry.
*3*  Clean the surface of the work with a damp sponge or kitchen paper and leave to dry.

## • finishing •

Apply an antique gold finish to the rim or moulding of the coaster as described on page 13. When dry, varnish as described on pages 13–14, taking care that the varnish doesn't run on the edges of the octagon. Varnish the inside also.

## • final touches •

Mark out the shape of the coaster on to the paper backing of some self-adhesive suede velvet and cut to fit the base of the coaster. This provides a professional finish and also protects furniture.

*NESTLING IN THE GRASS against the foot of a country stile is an early nineteenth century tin hatbox decorated with roses on a powder blue painted background*

# EDWARDIAN-STYLE PICNIC ITEMS

*Inspiration for the blue work came while walking my dogs through the bluebell woods which surround my home. The beauty and vibrance of these simple wild flowers spreading in a soft carpet through the trees was enchanting, their colour becoming almost fluorescent in the fading evening light. I came to a place in the wood where a young, windblown wild cherry sapling had become intertwined with ivy forming a natural bower and I began to imagine a romantic Edwardian picnic in this particularly lovely spot. Having finished their meal my fantasy couple have wandered deeper into the wood leaving their things behind – what a lovely thought! And how the mind wanders! The very simple pieces incorporated in the picnic are dealt with in the following pages. (Isn't the parasol gorgeous?)*

*The biscuit barrel has been painted midnight blue and given a simple design of hydrangeas in shades of blue and green which mingle beautifully with the background. Very simple to cut. The waisted jug has another basic design of full white hyacinths and an iris. The dear little milk-can opposite, and the old funnel and the Edwardian jug on page 51, were all found in local junk shops and were prepared using a brighter blue paint for the background colour. The step-by-step instructions are applicable to each item.*

*SOFT BLUES and greens in the hydrangeas blend into the midnight-blue background of this biscuit tin*

*(Opposite) A FANTASY Edwardian picnic in an enchanted bluebell wood*

| ◆ *materials list* ◆ |
| --- |

**VARIOUS EDWARDIAN-STYLE PICNIC ITEMS**

**PREPARATION**
Red oxide metal primer
An old 2.5cm (1 inch) brush
White spirit
Kitchen roll

**PAINTING**
250ml tin midnight (or navy) blue vinyl matt
   emulsion
2.5cm (1 inch) brush

**DÉCOUPAGE**
Good quality wrapping paper
Small sharp scissors
Craft knife
Wallpaper adhesive
Glue brush
Pasting board
Small sponge or kitchen paper

**ANTIQUE GOLD**
Small tubes of Gold and Raw Umber artists'
   acrylics
No. 4 artist's brush
Lidded container or jar
Water to mix

**VARNISHING**
Takcloth
Small tin of semi-matt varnish or polyurethane
   lacquer
2.5cm (1 inch) brush

### ◆ *preparation* ◆

1   Prepare each item as described on pages 15–18. If the item is to be functional, do not apply red oxide primer to the inner surfaces.

2   When the red oxide metal primer is completely dry, apply at least three coats of dark blue emulsion paint – it is water based and fast drying. Allow each coat to dry before applying the next. The dark blue finish should look perfect and dense, remember to turn the item upside down to paint the base.

### ◆ *découpage* ◆

1   Choose a few of the loveliest blooms and cut them out. You may find it easier to hold the base of the item in your lap while you are trying out different designs.

2   When you have selected the cutouts you wish to use, turn each one face down on the pasting board and spread the adhesive evenly over the entire surface ensuring the edges are covered. Turn right side up using a craft knife and apply to the item. Work out air bubbles, blemishes and excess glue with your fingers and when the paper is flat, press down the edges. Wipe away glue with damp kitchen paper. Allow to dry.

3   Clean up the surface of the work with a small damp sponge working from the centre of the design outwards, cleaning the background at the same time. Leave to dry.

### ◆ *finishing* ◆

Apply an antique gold finish to the container rims as described on page 13. Leave to dry, then varnish as described on pages 13–14.

▶ *COOL WHITE snowdrops decorate small items painted in deep blue. They look well painted in dark Chinese blue with a delicate but clear design in snowdrops. I hand-painted the lovely old bellied jug in the picture with acrylics and filled it with the darkest bluebells that I could find to complement the painting. Assembled on a crisp white antique linen cloth, the white reflected in the wild wreath of fresh clematis on the wall behind completes the blue and white theme*

# CAMEO BOX AND CANDLESTICK

*Having been an admirer of fine porcelain for many years, and a collector of English porcelain for a few, I began to look closely at the decoration on particular pieces. So often the flowers are hand-painted on a white background within a gilded 'frame' which is surrounded by another colour, like a cameo. Many plates are decorated in this way and I thought it would be fun to transpose the idea on to a couple of small items using découpage instead of hand-painting.*

## • *materials list* •

**SMALL WOODEN BOX AND CANDLESTICK**

**PREPARATION**
Fine-grade sandpaper or glasspaper

**PAINTING**
Small tin of white acrylic primer undercoat
250ml tin of bright mid- or turquoise blue matt
   emulsion
2.5cm (1 inch) or smaller brush

**CAMEO WORK**
White acrylic primer undercoat as above
Sample pot of ivory or pale cream emulsion
No. 4 artist's brush
Piece of white chalk

**ANTIQUE GOLD**
Small tubes of Gold and Raw Umber artists'
   acrylics
No. 4 artist's brush
Lidded container or jar
Water to mix

**DÉCOUPAGE**
Good quality wrapping paper with tiny blooms
Small sharp scissors
Craft knife
Wallpaper paste
Glue brush
Pasting board
Small sponge or kitchen paper

**VARNISHING**
Takcloth
Small tin of semi-matt or gloss varnish or
   polyurethane lacquer
2.5cm (1 inch) or smaller brush

**FINAL TOUCHES**
Small piece of self-adhesive suede velvet
Kitchen scissors

## • *preparation* •

1  Sand the entire box using fine sandpaper until smooth. Sand the candlestick by holding the sandpaper in the palm of your hand and working round it from top to bottom. Remove dust and apply two or three coats of white acrylic primer undercoat until the finish is perfect, allowing it to dry between coats.

2  Paint both items blue applying at least two coats for

◄ *DÉCOUPAGE imitates antique porcelain*

good all over cover and leave to dry.

3  Draw the cameos with white chalk; this will allow mistakes to be removed easily until the cameos are the right shape and evenly spaced.

4  Block in the shapes with acrylic primer undercoat allowing it to dry between coats. There should be no blue showing through. Apply two or three coats of the ivory or pale cream paint. All the paint is water based and will dry quickly so this is not the lengthy procedure it seems!

5  Outline the cameos in antique gold (see page 13). Mix a portion of the colour with a little water and hand-paint a faint thin line to the edges of the white. Balance the shape up as you go along – this can be done by widening the line or adding little dots, rope design or anything you find easy to apply. (Refer to pages 22–5 for hand-painted touches.)

6  When the cameos are dry and you are satisfied with their shape, paint one or two of the candlestick moulding bands gold for a more decorative look. Leave to dry.

## • *découpage* •

1  Cut a few of the smallest flowers and buds to fit within the shapes.

2  Turn each paper cutout face down on to the pasting board and brush the paste evenly over the surface and over the edges. Turn right side up using a craft knife and apply to the surface. Work out air and excess glue with your fingers, press down edges. Leave to dry out.

3  Clean off excess glue from the paper and the background with a dampened sponge or kitchen paper. Leave to dry. Remove dust with a takcloth in preparation for varnishing.

## • *finishing* •

Varnish the pieces as described on pages 13–14. Brush varnish out of the mouldings on the candlestick where it will collect and yellow.

## • *final touches* •

Cut out suitably sized pieces of self-adhesive suede and attach to the undersides of both box and candlestick.

# 5

# VIBRANT WORK

For the first three projects in this chapter I have used papers designed and hand-painted by Sandra Wall-Armitage which are marvellously bright and vibrant in colour, the tulips and iris in particular. The blossom paper provides a true test of cutting and is very definitely advanced découpage! The lovely sweet-pea paper (origin unknown) was wrapped around a birthday gift. The tulip paper provides a wonderful splash of colour on any background and if used with a little flair the flowers really come to life.

• • • •

*BRILLIANTLY COLOURED*
*tulips cut with a little*
*imagination look wonderful*
*on almost any background*

# TUMULTUOUS TULIPS – JUG AND BOX

*This design is bright and cheerful and would look super in a modern setting or as a focal point in a plainly
decorated room. Both the jug and box are old, the deedbox dates back to the mid-nineteenth century and the jug
is probably 1940s, but given the same treatment this is no longer apparent.
The lovely warm cream background provides a good neutral base on which to show up the brilliant colours of
the tulips to their best advantage. (Black looks stunning too.) The paper needs to be used imaginatively. By
tucking short stems underneath the preceding row of flower heads and cutting extra stems to balance them, a
natural effect will emerge. Sometimes they appear to be swaying in the breeze.*

## • materials list •

**TINWARE JUG AND BOX**
**PREPARATION**
Red oxide metal primer
An old 2.5cm (1 inch) brush
White spirit
Kitchen paper
**PAINTING**
250ml tin of warm cream vinyl silk or vinyl
  matt emulsion
2.5cm (1 inch) brush
**DÉCOUPAGE**
Brightly coloured hand-painted paper with tulip
  design
Small sharp scissors
Craft knife
Wallpaper adhesive

Glue brush  •  Pasting board
Small sponge or kitchen paper
**ANTIQUE GOLD**
Small tubes of Gold and Raw Umber artists'
  acrylics
No. 4 artist's brush
Lidded container or jar
Water to mix
**VARNISHING**
Takcloth
Small tin of semi-matt craft varnish
2.5cm (1 inch) brush
**FINAL TOUCHES**
Suitably sized piece of self-adhesive suede
  velvet for base of box
Kitchen scissors

## • preparation •

1  Prepare the items as described on pages 15–18.
2  When the red oxide metal primer is completely dry,
apply at least two coats of white acrylic primer undercoat
allowing the first coat to dry before applying the second.
It may be necessary to paint a third coat.
3  For the topcoat apply two coats of warm cream vinyl
silk or vinyl matt emulsion.

## • découpage •

1  Cut out blocks of flowers, leaves and stems, removing all unnecessary background. Lay the flowers on a
sheet of white paper or a tabletop to get an idea of the
type of design you would like to make.
2  Begin by pasting and sticking the underneath pieces
first. A craft knife is useful for lifting small pasted
cutouts from the pasting board. Reshape where neces-

sary and cut extra stems and leaves for a logical balanced
design.
3  When the design is completed leave to dry thoroughly before cleaning off the excess glue with a
dampened sponge.

## • finishing •

Apply an antique gold finish to the rim of the jug, the
rim of the box lid and base, and the box's handles and
escutcheon as described on page 13. Leave to dry, then
varnish as described on pages 13–14. Prop the lid of the
box open to avoid sticking.

## • final touches •

It is a good idea to attach some self-adhesive suede velvet
to the underside of the box to protect your furniture from
damage.

# BLUE IRIS CHURN

*A redundant 10-gallon milk churn has been painted an eye-catching bright blue and decorated with huge irises which appear to be 'growing' from its base. It would look fantastic filled with walking sticks and umbrellas in a dark hall or, with its lid replaced, as a pedestal for a jardinière to display a wonderful arrangement of flowers. A thoroughly conspicuous, attractive and unusual piece.*

*Many farmers will gladly sell their milk churns, now made redundant by milk-tankers. Check first that they actually have a base, that the lid will come off and that the whole thing isn't eaten away with rust! The more recent aluminium ones like this one do not have the character of the old pitted iron churns embossed with the farmer's name or that of the dairy, but are well worth decorating*

## ◆ *materials list* ◆

**MILK CHURN**
**PREPARATION**
Wire brush if the churn is rusty
Red oxide metal primer
An old 2.5cm (1 inch) brush
White spirit
Kitchen paper
**PAINTING**
Small tin of white acrylic primer undercoat
250ml tin or similar of blue vinyl silk emulsion
   or colour of your choice
2.5cm (1 inch) brush
**DÉCOUPAGE**
6 sheets of hand-painted paper with blue irises
   or other long stemmed flowers

Small sharp scissors
Craft knife
Wallpaper adhesive
Pasting board ◆ Glue brush
Small sponge or kitchen paper
**HAND-PAINTED DECORATION**
Either a small tube of artists' acrylic or a 250ml
   tin of matt emulsion paint in a colour of your
   choice to complement the topcoat
No. 5 artist's brush
**VARNISHING**
Takcloth
Small tin of semi-matt pale craft varnish
2.5cm (1 inch) brush
White spirit

## ◆ *preparation* ◆

*1*  Prepare the churn as described on pages 15–18.
*2*  When the red oxide metal primer is completely dry, apply at least two coats of white acrylic primer, allowing the first coat to dry before applying the second.
*3*  Apply topcoat in a colour of your choice. The churn in the photograph has been painted in a lovely blue to complement the iris pattern.

## ◆ *découpage* ◆

*1*  The paper for this project has large motifs and is easy to cut but the overall design has to be considered first and worked out carefully. The simplest method is to measure around the circumference of the base of the churn, then transfer the measurement on to a tabletop. The cut flowers can be laid down on the table into a design. When the 'join' is reached extra filling-in may

be necessary to tie the whole thing together. If possible stand the churn on the table to enable you to work at eye level and in a more comfortable position.
*2*  Paste and apply the cutouts, working out any excess glue or air bubbles from the centre outwards. A craft knife is helpful for lifting smaller cutouts.
*3*  Allow to dry thoroughly, then clean off the excess glue from the background and surface of the découpage using a damp sponge or kitchen paper.

## ◆ *finishing* ◆

Pick out the rim and handles in a complementary colour using a No. 5 brush (violet has been used for the churn illustrated). Leave to dry, then varnish as described on pages 13–14.

▶ *BLUE Iris churn*

# BLOSSOM BUCKETS

*We continue the vibrant, springtime theme of the previous pages with a project involving very advanced cutting and pasting techniques. If you feel sufficiently confident to meet the challenge, find your sharpest, most pointed scissors and have a go!*
*Filled to overflowing with cow parsley which covers many a verge and roadside or the later guelder roses or of course blossom of any kind, these buckets can be used for a floorstanding arrangement or in a fireplace, in a corner or perhaps on a hall table.*
*The blossom-covered paper was hand-painted by Sandra Wall-Armitage.*

THE COLOURS *are reversed on this galvanized bucket*

BLOSSOM CASCADES *from the top of an Edwardian slop-bucket*

## ◆ materials list ◆

**METAL BUCKET, ENAMELLED IF POSSIBLE**
**PREPARATION**
Red oxide metal primer
An old 2.5cm (1 inch) brush
White spirit
Kitchen paper
**PAINTING**
Small tin of white acrylic primer undercoat
Small tin of white or lime green vinyl silk
   emulsion for the topcoat
250ml tin of white or Spring Lily (or other
   bright Acid Green) emulsion for the sponging
2.5cm (1 inch) brush
Small sea-sponge
**DÉCOUPAGE**
Blossom-covered paper (the one shown was
   hand-painted by Sandra Wall-Armitage)
Small sharp scissors
Craft knife
Wallpaper adhesive
Glue brush
Pasting board
Small sponge
**HAND-PAINTED DECORATION**
Small tubes of Gold and Raw Umber artists'
   acrylics **or** a darker green paint could be used
   instead
Lidded container or jar
Water to mix
**VARNISHING**
Takcloth
Small tin of the palest semi-matt craft varnish
2.5cm (1 inch) brush

## ◆ preparation ◆

1   Prepare the bucket as described on pages 15–18. For galvanized items see page 18.

2   When the red oxide metal primer is completely dry, apply three coats of white acrylic primer undercoat, allowing each coat to dry before applying the next.

3   Apply two or more coats of your chosen top colour until the finish is perfect (allow to dry between coats).

4   A sponged on finish should now be applied. You could follow the description on page 20, but I was extremely lazy with the sponging and in each case I dipped the tip of a dampened sponge directly into the

250ml tin (Acid Green on the white bucket and white sponged on the green bucket). The pattern of the sponging took the shape of wisteria or lilac cascading down from the rim of the bucket – as does the découpage design. The inside of each bucket has been sponged from the top rim also, quite sparsely. Allow to dry.

## ◆ découpage ◆

1   This is very advanced cutting but the results, as you see, are very rewarding. Cut out blocks of leaves and blossom that would naturally hang downwards. For the minutely detailed cutting out in between petals make an incision with the pointed tip of one of the scissor blades first. If a stem is particularly difficult (and many are) cut straight through it and butt it together when you paste it on.

2   Paste evenly over the back of the cutout pieces taking the glue over the edges on to the pasting board. If this proves too difficult you could apply as an alternative the glue to the surface of the bucket. Use a craft knife to assist in removing the cutouts from the pasting board and to position them on the bucket. (It is a good idea to rinse the glue from your fingers every so often, otherwise the surface of the paper will come off.)

3   A few of the larger leaves can be arranged around the top rim of the bucket last of all, to help balance the design and to give the impression of hanging foliage. Small leaf decorations can be stuck inside the top rim of the bucket to finish it off.

4   When all the design is stuck on, leave it to dry out before cleaning off the excess glue from the work with a damp sponge or kitchen paper.

## ◆ finishing ◆

Apply an antique gold finish to the handle, rim and base of the bucket as described on page 13. On a green bucket you may prefer to pick out the features with a darker leaf-green paint. Allow to dry, then varnish as described on pages 13–14.

(Overleaf) THE EDWARDIAN *handled bucket is sponged a fresh new-leaf-green on to a white background to make a perfect backdrop for the design of lilac and apple blossom. Inside are a few ivy leaves. The second bucket is of the modern galvanized variety and more squat in shape, but treated in a reverse paint effect (ie green background with white sponging) and finished in green rather than gilded. They make a pretty pair!*

# LETTER RACK

HAND-PAINTED LETTER RACK *Hand-coloured photocopies may be used instead of wrapping paper for the découpage design. This letter rack was decorated with photocopied line drawings which were cut out and pasted on. Once dry they were hand-painted with acrylics using them thickly like oil-paint. This is an easy and quick way of decorating small items. (For suppliers of such items see page 143.)*

# SWEET PEA CACHEPOT AND BOX

*This cachepot makes an attractive holder for one or more flower pots which will brighten any kitchen or conservatory. The materials required for the tin are exactly the same as for the cachepot, and the sweet pea design is applied in almost the same way. A grouping of blooms has been applied to the lid top in the shape of an oval. The rims, keyhole and handles have been gilded and the underneath baized.*

## ♦ materials list ♦

**METAL CACHEPOT**
**PREPARATION**
Red oxide metal primer
An old 2.5cm (1 inch) brush
White spirit
Kitchen paper
**PAINTING**
Small tin of white acrylic primer undercoat
250ml tins of soft green and pale blue vinyl
    matt emulsion (or a slate colour)
2.5cm (1 inch) brush
**DÉCOUPAGE**
Paper depicting sweet peas
Small sharp scissors
Craft knife
Wallpaper adhesive
Glue brush
Pasting board
Small sponge or kitchen paper
**ANTIQUE GOLD**
Small tubes of Gold and Raw Umber artists'
    acrylics
No. 4 artist's brush
Lidded container or jar
Water to mix
**VARNISHING**
Takcloth
Small tin of semi-matt craft varnish
2.5cm (1 inch) brush

## ♦ preparation ♦

*1*   Prepare tinware as described on pages 15–18. For zinc or galvanized items see page 18.
*2*   When the red oxide is completely dry, apply at least two coats of white primer undercoat allowing it to dry between coats.
*3*   For the top coat apply two coats of a soft slate colour

(or soft blue and green painted on with one brush dipping it first into blue and then into green without cleaning), taking care over the handles and the scalloped edge where the paint will collect and run both inside and out.

## ♦ découpage ♦

*1*   Cut out the curling stems with care as their shape and form will enhance the decoration. If you find them difficult to handle – especially to paste, the stems can be cut at intervals and butted together when they are stuck on the cachepot.
*2*   Turn each cutout face down on the pasting board and brush on the paste evenly ensuring the edges are covered. Turn right side up using the craft knife and position on the cachepot. (Don't panic if a design curls up, just uncurl it gently.)
*3*   When the decoration is finished leave it to dry out, then clean the excess glue from the background and the surface of the decoration working carefully with a damp sponge or kitchen paper.

## ♦ finishing ♦

Apply an antique gold finish to the scalloped edge of the cachepot as described on page 13 – remember to neaten the inside too. Leave to dry. Paint the bottom rim and the handles in the same way and allow to dry. Finally, varnish as described on pages 13–14. Brush out any runs on the scalloped edge and where the handles join the body of the cachepot. Approximately 10 coats should be sufficient for the outside and unless there is a great difference in the colour, two or three coats should be enough for the inside.

*(Overleaf)* SWEET PEA CACHEPOT *A pretty summery decoration of sweet peas entwines its way around a fluted cachepot. The background is streaked in two colours of matt emulsion paint: a soft green and a pale blue combine in places to make a lovely aquamarine. The box has a similar decoration*

# *6*

# *FURNITURE*

It is very rewarding to transform a shabby piece of furniture completely. One sometimes hears of suitable pieces languishing at the back of a garage or garden shed, stored in a barn or occasionally thrown out! They may have had a little woodworm or damage, or possibly have become unfashionable. Auction sales and junk shops are another source of second-hand furniture ripe for simple restoration. Stripping is sometimes necessary, but often only painting is needed. Don't dismiss reproduction pieces as they can be made to look old; the main criterion is a good shape.

◆ ◆ ◆ ◆

## VICTORIAN PINE CUPBOARD

*A good old country cupboard which would have originated as a wall cupboard in a large high-ceilinged Victorian kitchen. The body of the cupboard is painted in a bright leaf-green emulsion and the front and side panels have been sponged in three colours in a diagonal flowing movement. The découpage decoration has been 'mirrored' on the two panels. This idea could be used on wardrobe doors in the right setting.*

> ◆ *materials list* ◆
>
> **DOUBLE-DOORED WOODEN CUPBOARD**
> **PREPARATION**
> 100 grade sandpaper
> **PAINTING**
> White acrylic primer undercoat
> 2.5cm (1 inch) brush
> 250ml tin of leaf-green emulsion
> Small tin of white vinyl silk emulsion
> Sample pot of palest grey matt emulsion
> Small tube of Payne's Grey artists' acrylic (optional)
> Small Unibond/PVA adhesive
> Lidded container and small carton
> Natural sea-sponge
> **DÉCOUPAGE**
> 6 sheets of good quality wrapping paper
>
> Small sharp scissors  ◆  Craft knife
> Wallpaper paste  ◆  Glue brush
> Pasting boards  ◆  Piece of white chalk
> Tape measure  ◆  Small sponge or kitchen paper
> **HAND-PAINTED DECORATION**
> Small tube of Venetian Red artists' acrylic
> No. 8 artist's brush  ◆  Water to mix
> **VARNISHING**
> Small tin of semi-matt varnish or polyurethane
>    lacquer
> 2.5cm (1 inch) brush  ◆  Takcloth
> Fine-grade sandpaper  ◆  White spirit
> **TO POLISH THE CUPBOARD**
> Natural beeswax, gedgewax or white wax polish and
> soft cloth (see page 83)

▶ *HUGE ROSES adorn an old Victorian cupboard. The old Victorian hatbox I hand-painted with wild dog roses; it fits well into the charming setting of a rose-covered porchway at the home of a friend*

◆

### • *preparation* •

*1*  If your cupboard is of stripped wood prepare it by sanding thoroughly in the same direction as the grain. If your piece is painted or stained, treat as described on pages 14–15.

*2*  Remove dust; apply the first coat of primer under-coat and let it dry. Run your hand over the surface and edges and if there are rough patches remaining rub it down again. When you are satisfied the surface is smooth to the touch apply the second coat and let it dry. Paint the cupboard with two or three coats until the surface looks near perfect in its undercoat.

*3*  Topcoat with two or three coats of leaf-green emulsion, remembering to leave the side and door panels white. Leave to dry.

*4*  Apply two coats of white vinyl silk emulsion to the panels and let them dry.

*5*  Mix one tablespoon of the leaf-green emulsion paint with sufficient white vinyl silk emulsion to lighten it. Then mix an emulsion glaze by combining one table-spoon of PVA/Unibond, one tablespoon of the paler green paint mix and approximately three tablespoons of water. On the lid place a little pale grey matt emulsion, a portion of white vinyl silk and a small squeeze of Payne's Grey.

*6*  Squeeze the sea-sponge out in clean water and remove excess moisture. Dip the tip of the sponge into the green glaze and with light dabbing movements work at an angle, diagonally, leaving two or three spaces in which to sponge on the soft grey. Leave to dry. For the second sponging the green can be built up a little more and white added to the sponge in some places, and a touch of Payne's Grey for added interest. When you are happy with the finish add the lines of soft grey and leave it all to dry completely.

### • *découpage* •

*1*  Cut out a selection of lovely large blooms, some with buds and interesting stamens, fine curling stems, thorns, etc; a good variety will add interest and depth to the design. Have plenty of leaves to look as natural as possible and aim to choose colours which will blend with the background or the overall colour scheme.

*2*  A low cupboard can be laid on its back to make designing easier, but assuming the cupboard is upright, cut for one door only and decorate it first. It might be helpful to hold the cutouts against the panel and mark their outlines with chalk.

*3*  Turn each cutout face down on the board and paste evenly all over ensuring the edges are covered. Using a craft knife, turn right side up and position on the panel, taking extra care to work out air bubbles and excess glue which is always a problem with large flowers. Press from the centre outwards with a rolling finger movement, wiping the glue away with damp kitchen roll. **Stand back and look** occasionally as it is impossible to see the overall design when you are right on top of it.

*4*  Before decorating the second door panel it is a good idea to measure the margins around the design and where the largest and most noticeable blooms are. Chalk around the shapes again to help position the cutouts correctly. You will have to dissect the flowers and leaves and reshape them in order for them to appear as a mirror image and it will be necessary to fill in with the odd leaf and bud to balance the picture.

*5*  When both panels are finished allow the work to dry out before cleaning off the excess glue from the back-ground and the decoration with a damp sponge or kitchen paper.

### • *finishing* •

Mix a small amount of Venetian Red with a little water and draw a steady straight line around the inside edge of the panels. Keep some damp kitchen paper by your side to wipe off smudges and mistakes. Allow to dry completely, then varnish the panels as described on pages 13–14. Apply at least 10 coats.

(*NOTE*  It is not necessary to varnish the frame as emulsion can be wax polished to a satin-like patina using a soft cloth. Do this only when the varnish is completely dry.)

# COMMODE

COMMODE *Made of oak, this little commode was found in an antique and second-hand shop. I thought it would be fun to decorate it as a box and to use with the lid open to display flowers. The commode was rubbed down with 100 grade sandpaper, the rotten wood by the old hinges was repaired and filled and new hinges fitted. It was first given two coats of flat varnish to stop the dark stain bleeding into the paint, then painted in dark red emulsion and 'streaked' to add depth and interest, by brushing Payne's Grey acrylic over the wet red emulsion and leaving the brush marks. The découpage decoration is cut from another favourite paper and the mixture of fruit and flowers is a little different. For the front panel I used vine leaves from another paper to give a three-dimensional look. The little hand-painted leaves on the top balance the design. The decoration is under approximately 15 coats of varnish.*

# DEMI-LUNE TABLE

*The elegant lines of this pretty little table have been accentuated by the display of two tall candlestick lamps and a profusion of pink roses underneath an antique mirror, making a most attractive feature in a hall which can be tucked into the smallest space.*

*It is a reproduction which has been decorated to look like an old table. The cameo effect is simple to do with two colours of paint and a steady hand! The delicate floral decoration is découpage and requires some meticulously fine cutting, although different flowers could be chosen. The table has been aged with an antique and craquelure finish.*

## • *materials list* •

**DEMI-LUNE TABLE**
**PREPARATION**
100 grade sandpaper
**PAINTING**
White acrylic primer undercoat
2.5cm (1 inch) brush
Small tin of Gardenia vinyl silk emulsion
Small tin of soft green emulsion (or colour of
   your choice)
No. 4 artist's brush
**DÉCOUPAGE**
Good quality paper covered in tiny delicate
   flowers
Small sharp scissors
Craft knife
Wallpaper adhesive
Glue brush
Pasting board
Small sponge or kitchen paper
**HAND-PAINTED DECORATION**
Small tubes of Gold and Raw Umber artists'
   acrylics
No. 3 or 4 coachlining brush
Lidded jar or container
Water to mix
**VARNISHING**
Takcloth
Small tin of semi-matt pale varnish
   or polyurethane lacquer
2.5cm (1 inch) brush
Fine-grade sandpaper
White spirit
**CRAQUELURE**
Materials as listed on page 25

## • *preparation* •

*1*   Sand the table if necessary to provide a 'key' for the paint. Apply two or three coats of fast-drying acrylic primer undercoat allowing each coat to dry before applying the next. Wash brush thoroughly in soap and water to use again for the topcoat.

*2*   Apply at least two coats of Gardenia vinyl silk emulsion for a good all-over cover to all surfaces except the front panels. It is often a good idea to turn the table upside down to begin, painting as much as possible before turning it back the right way up to complete the coat of paint. Leave to dry.

*3*   Paint the front panels in soft green emulsion.

*4*   Mark out faintly the shape of the cameos on to the top and front of the table using very pale, weak green

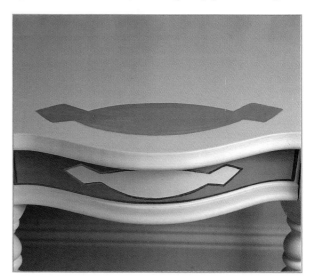

*CAMEO shapes before outlining*

▶ *PAINTING and découpage combine to decorate an elegant demi-lune*

paint, mistakes can be wiped off using dampened kitchen roll. You may well have several attempts to get the shape right but this is quite usual. (Alternatively you could trace the shape on page 73 as a guideline.)

5   Paint the cameo shapes with an art brush. You will require a few coats to get a solid colour; don't worry if the edges are not perfect, they can be improved when the cameo is outlined. Have a piece of kitchen paper handy to erase mistakes.

6   Now coachline the cameos using antique gold, mixed as described on page 13. Cover the coachliner evenly without overloading it; place the tip of the brush on the beginning of a line and pull the brush towards you, when the paint runs out, replenish and continue with the outline. Take care to replace the tip of the brush on to the gold line, overlapping a little; remove mistakes and smudges quickly with damp kitchen paper.

### • *découpage* •

1   The choice of design is yours; small posies or a centrally positioned group of tiny blooms would look just as attractive as the delicate flowers and stems used in the photograph. Cut out a good selection paying great attention to detail and accuracy. Begin by placing the cutouts on the tabletop to fill in the three cameos until they look balanced. Stand back and look! If your design is positioned centrally chalk around the edges of the cutouts which will be helpful when they are replaced after pasting. The fine stemmy design was pasted on in sections without the aid of chalk marks as they would have been thicker than the stems themselves!

2   To paste, turn each cutout face down on the board and brush the glue evenly over the surface ensuring the edges are covered. Use a craft knife to ease the fragile cutouts gently from the board and to position them on the table. Rinse your fingers occasionally to avoid taking the surface off the paper. Press the cutouts down when all the blemishes have been removed. When the decoration is complete leave to dry.

3   When all three cameos on the top of the table have been completed, check that they look balanced. If not, fill in any gaps by adding the odd leaf or stem until it is pleasing to the eye. Decorate the remainder in exactly the same way. Leave to dry out.

4   Clean up the work carefully using either a slightly dampened sponge or kitchen paper. Should any fine stem become loose or dislodged, re-stick down. Remove all excess glue from the surface of the table so that it is perfectly clean and free from dust. The table is now ready to varnish.

### • *finishing* •

As the table is to have an antique and craquelure finish, apply a thin coat of varnish *to the cameos only* just to seal the paper cutouts. Leave to dry, then apply the craquelure and ageing varnish as described on pages 25–6.

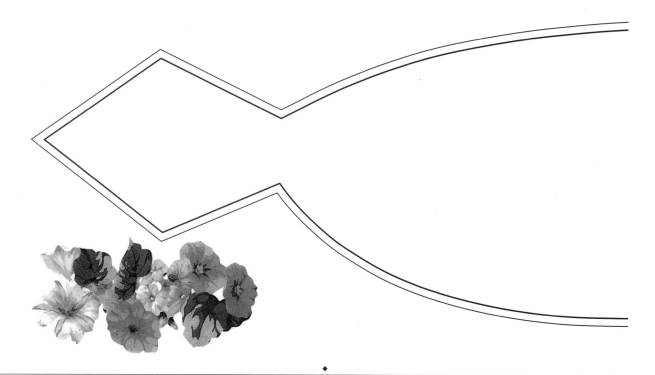

CAMEOS *outlined in antique gold frame the finely cut flowers*

TRACE *the cameo shapes onto the table using the pattern provided*

# FLORENTINE BUREAU AND BALLOON BACK CHAIR

*Both the oak bureau and the Victorian balloon back chair were bought cheaply at auction sales. The bureau was in very poor condition, having many gouges and cuts which, to make matters worse, had been filled with wall filler quite unsuitable for wood! What a challenge!*
*The delicate balloon back tucks into a corner of my small study and doubles well as an extra occasional or dining chair when friends descend.*
*Both have been painted in black emulsion and decorated in a Florentine design paper taken from a seventeenth-century tabletop on which the grapes were mother of pearl.*

## ◆ materials list ◆

**BUREAU AND CHAIR**

**PREPARATION**

100 grade sandpaper or aluminium oxide (80 grade for hard oak only)
180 grade sandpaper or aluminium oxide
240 grade sandpaper
Sanding block
Soft cloth
Water based wood filler or stopper
Filling knife
Small tin of natural beeswax or gedgewax polish and soft cloth to apply (if drawers should not run freely)

**PAINTING**

500ml tin of black vinyl matt emulsion
2.5cm (1 inch) brush

**DÉCOUPAGE**

8 sheets of Florentine wrapping paper
Small sharp scissors
Craft knife

Wallpaper adhesive
Small glue brush ◆ Pasting board
Small sponge or kitchen paper
Piece of white chalk

**ANTIQUE GOLD**

Small tubes of Gold and Raw Umber artists' acrylics
No. 5 artist's brush
Lidded container or jar
Water to mix

**VARNISHING**

Takcloth
Small tin of semi-matt varnish or polyurethane lacquer
2.5cm (1 inch) brush
Fine-grade sandpaper
White spirit

**TO POLISH THE BUREAU AND CHAIR**

Natural beeswax or white wax polish or gedgewax and a soft cloth; see page 83

▶ *A RUSTIC OAK bureau and Victorian balloon back chair decorated as a pair for a small study*

### • *preparing the bureau* •

If your piece is painted you may find the services of a professional furniture stripping company, who usually collect and deliver, well worth while for the amount of effort it saves. If you tackle the job yourself, an electric power sander will cut your work in half, but there is no reason why most pieces cannot be done by hand. If your furniture is painted please turn to page 15 for preparation of wood in the paint.

*1* Remove all handles and decorative attachments if possible and remove the drawers. Clean off any damaged leather or paper lining in the top of the desk by soaking it off with water. Fill chips, holes and deep scratches in the wood with a water-based wood stopper or plastic wood.

*2a* **Hand sanding** Cut the abrasive sheet into quarters and wrap it around the sanding block. Do not fold the sheet into four otherwise the abrasive surfaces will be facing one another and will wear out quickly. If you prefer you may use the whole sheet with the flat of your hand, but it is more difficult to keep a grip. Sand your piece down, keeping an even pressure and always sanding in the same direction as the grain in the wood. Pay particular attention to the edges of the desk and those of the lid and drawers. When the surface begins to feel smooth to the touch, wipe it with a damp cloth following the grain to remove the dust and avoid clogging and to raise the grain for the next sanding.

*2b* **Power sanding** If you have an orbital sander you could use aluminium oxide with a medium paper backing but if it is a disc or drum sander, cloth-backed aluminium oxide may last longer. Alternatively the appropriate sandpaper can be used to fit your particular type of machine.

Always sand in the same direction as the grain in the wood and pay particular attention to the edges of the desk and those of the drawers and the lid. It is worth smoothing the edges of drawers to protect fine articles which may be stored in them. When the surface is even, and all cuts and chips are removed, run your fingers over it and if it feels smooth switch off the sander and wipe over the surface with a damp cloth to remove the dust and avoid clogging – this will also open up the grain for the next sanding.

*3* Keep renewing the piece of sandpaper if you are using a sanding block, and knock it occasionally to avoid clogging. Take the 180 grit abrasive and begin the whole process again, running your hand frequently over the wood to get a good indication of how it is progressing and where imperfections remain. When it is finished remove the dust with a brush or damp cloth. The surface needs a 'key' on which to paint, it does not require fine sanding.

*4* Replace the drawers to see if they run smoothly; if they stick, a minor adjustment is necessary. Using 240 grit abrasive, hand sand the top and bottom edges of the drawer(s) which should glide along the runners. With a soft cloth apply a good measure of wax polish, rubbing the edges. Leave for five minutes, then sand the polish into the edges until the surface is satin smooth (this happens quickly). When the drawers are finished, leave them out of the frame for painting.

### • *painting the bureau* •

As black is a difficult colour to work on if the light is inadequate, find an angle-lamp or spotlight as it will be impossible to see into the small sections in the top of the bureau. Remove debris and dust before you apply the

first coat of black emulsion. Paint the inside top and lid and let it dry. Paint the frame and the drawer fronts and leave to dry. Apply two or three more coats until the overall cover is good, and let it dry. Replace handles, lock and escutcheons.

## • *découpage* •

*1* The Florentine paper is tricky to cut, but fortunately the background is the same colour as the paint and if a little of the background remains it will not be noticeable. The curling stems and grapes can be cut out in sections as they are fragile to paste and stick; they can then be butted together to form one continuous length when they are stuck to the surface of the bureau.

*2* Draw a faint chalk mark to indicate the shape and position of the design on the bureau. Cut a good selection of grapes and fruit so that you have plenty to choose from for the decoration.

*3* To paste, turn each paper cutout singly face down on the board and brush the adhesive evenly over the surface. Use the craft knife to assist in lifting the cutout from the board and position on the bureau. Once in place, press down flat. Fingers require frequent washing as the excess glue will build up and remove the surface of the paper.

*4* When each section of the bureau is decorated leave it to dry out. **Stand back and look** occasionally to check if the design is balanced, equidistant from drawer handles, etc. Extra pieces can be cut to fill in where necessary.

*5* The inside of the flap of the oak bureau in the photograph was too chipped and uneven to decorate but was masked by self-adhesive black suede which was neatened by braiding the edges. The inside and top is decorated with fruit.

*6* When the decoration is dry, clean up the surface and background to remove excess glue with a damp sponge or kitchen paper. Let it dry.

## • *finishing* •

Remove dust with a takcloth. Take the drawers out of the desk to avoid sticking. Apply varnish as described on pages 13–14, brushing it out evenly to avoid runs. Varnish both inside and out. When the final coat has dried, leave for 24 hours until the varnish has hardened then apply beeswax polish, buffing with a soft cloth after 10 minutes. Repeat until a silky patina is achieved.

## • *florentine chair* •

The balloon back in the photograph is of mahogany with a lot of non-active worm holes (nothing will survive hot chemical stripping!).

*1* Turn the chair upside down on a working surface which is protected with a plastic sheet. Hand sand until smooth. Apply several coats of black emulsion both in this position and afterwards turning the chair upright. Let it dry between coats. Cut out a design of your choice and decorate the back and front of the frame using the same technique as for the bureau.

*2* As the chair is Victorian it is in keeping to decorate the pretty turned legs and spindle with antique gold as described on page 13.

*3* When the antique gold is dry, varnish carefully as before, applying only two coats to the lower parts, but at least 10 coats over the design on the front and back of the chair as it will be constantly touched and must be hardwearing.

*4* When the chair is absolutely dry, it can be upholstered, or re-covered quickly and easily by stretching a piece of calico or silk over the seat and stapling it underneath with a staple gun.

# 7

# THE SITTING-ROOM

*A* room in which to relax and enjoy life's peaceful pleasures: good conversation, reading, music. During the winter months it is an ideal place to gather around the fire for afternoon tea or to entertain friends in the evening. Why not make the coffee table (below) or screen (page 90) a special feature of the room? Decorated in an outstandingly beautiful design it will give you lasting pleasure.

•   •   •   •

## COFFEE TABLE

*This table is one of the most admired pieces of work I have ever produced. It literally stopped people in their tracks as they were passing my stand at the Country Living Fair, all enchanted by the huge full-blown roses on a sumptuous background which give it such a lifelike vibrance. One can almost touch the flowers and breathe in their scent. This is a fine example of the potential of paint-finishes, the use of colour and the versatility of découpage design.*

*This table is constructed from new pine with an MDF (medium density fibreboard) top which is a perfect surface on which to work and is available to order, see list of suppliers on page 143. It has been paint-finished to look like polished slate using the technique of three-colour sponging.*

*Another option would be to use a rich Chinese lacquer-red and decorate with bold flowers taken from a print of a Dutch masters painting, then apply an antique and craquelure finish (see pages 25–6) and gild fairly heavily (see page 13). Alternatively, paint black and decorate using a paper depicting the finest seventeenth-century Florentine design to make a border on the table top, applying many coats of varnish to make the grapes shine like mother of pearl. All quite different and varied pieces of work, and just a few examples of what can be achieved.*

*The pictured design of full-blown summer roses is under at least 25 layers of varnish. After approximately 20 coats it was rubbed down with the finest grade wire wool, the process being repeated between three or four subsequent coats in order to produce a good finish.*

*The table has been in constant use for three years and is polished regularly with white beeswax polish which improves the patina and renews the 'glow' and depth.*

▶ *BUTTERFLIES AND BUGS enhance the natural look of this flowered design*

## • materials list •

**COFFEE TABLE**

**PREPARATION**

1 sheet of 100 grade sandpaper (if the pine legs
   are rough) or 180 grade sandpaper

240 grade sandpaper

**PAINTING**

Small tin of white acrylic primer undercoat

Small tin of vinyl silk emulsion in a bright
   strong blue such as Dulux Regatta 2959-B or
   4060-B or a similar colour from another range

2.5cm (1 inch) brush

2 natural sea-sponges (or one large one cut up)

Wide necked plastic carton with lid

Old lids to use as palettes

Old spoon to measure paint

Container of clean water for washing sponges

Kitchen paper roll

Large tubes of white, Payne's Grey and
   Hooker's Green artists' acrylics

Small tube of black artists' acrylic

Small tin of Unibond/PVA

Water to mix

**DÉCOUPAGE**

Paper of your choice

Small sharp scissors

Craft knife

Wallpaper adhesive

Small glue brush

Pasting boards

Small sponge or kitchen paper

Piece of white chalk   •   Takcloth

**ANTIQUE GOLD**

Tubes of Gold and Raw Umber artists' acrylics

No. 5 artist's brush

Lidded container or jar   •   Water to mix

**VARNISHING**

Takcloth

Litre tin of clear gloss varnish or polyurethane
   lacquer and smallest tin of semi-matt

2.5cm (1 inch) brush

00 grade flour paper or glasspaper

0000 grade wire wool or black 'wet and dry'
   sandpaper 280 grade

White spirit

**TO POLISH THE TABLE**

Soft cloth

White gedgewax polish

## • preparation •

Preparation is particularly important to the success of
this project and time spent at this stage will be well
rewarded by the end result.

*1*   It is not uncommon for new pine in the raw to be
rough and therefore the legs may need sanding down
with 100 grade sandpaper. Sand in the same direction as
the grain, paying special attention to the edges. Change
to 180 grade for a finer finish, feeling the wood with your
fingers, smoothing your hand over the surface to detect
any further areas that need attention.

*2*   Feel the top surface and around the moulding on the
edges; if the MDF feels rough sand it with 180 grade
sandpaper. Remove dust and turn the table upside down
on to a workbench or a table (which can be protected by
a piece of plastic sheet) to save bending down.

*3*   Apply the first coat of acrylic primer undercoat to the
underside, legs and anything else that is visible, and
leave to dry. Turn the table upright and paint the
remainder, working in the direction of the grain (as the
top is MDF you will have to imagine that the grain
would run the length of the surface). Take care not to
clog up the moulded edges. Leave to dry.

*4*   With a piece of 240 grade sandpaper sand the table
down again until it is smooth. You may find it easier to
use a quarter of the sheet wrapped around a sanding
block to work on the table top. Remove the dust, apply
the second coat of acrylic primer undercoat and leave to
dry.

*5*   Continue along these lines until you are satisfied
with the look and feel of the table and a good all-over
cover has been achieved with the primer undercoat.

*6*   In the same way, but without sanding between coats,
apply two or three coats of the bright blue vinyl silk
emulsion for the topcoat which will receive the paint-
finish. Leave to dry.

*7*   In the base of a container measure out two tablespoons of bright blue paint, two tablespoons of Unibond/
PVA and between four and eight tablespoons of water
and mix together to make an emulsion glaze. On the
lid(s) squeeze out a good length of Payne's Grey,
Hooker's Green and the same of white with a smaller
amount of black.

8 Squeeze the sponges out in clean water and dab off excess water on kitchen paper. With the first sponge begin by dipping part of it into the blue emulsion glaze and part of it into the Payne's Grey and apply at random on to the surface building up areas of colour. Next try the blue glaze with some of the green and white and so on, mainly working up from dark to light and working to cover a quite substantial part of the top of the table, sides, legs, etc. Build up the colours until the sponges are full of paint and they will eventually begin to merge. Leave to dry out for a time and wash the sponges for the next attempt. Replenish the colours on the palette when necessary. Repeat the process and make alterations in the colour as you go along; if the base colour is dark, by using white with the dark colours and pressing the sponge quite hard, 'depth' will begin to appear. Sponge the whole table walking around it and standing back to look at it constantly to ensure complete coverage. When you are pleased with the result leave it to dry for several hours. (See also page 20 for picture showing how to build up the colours for polished slate finish.)

You may need to rinse out the sponges once or twice and your hands and nails will be covered in emulsion glaze but this will clean off with soap and water. Remember to wash the sponges out finally in soap and water and leave them in cold water to recover for a while.

### • *découpage* •

1 Cut out several large blooms, a collection of buds and interesting leaves, especially if they have dewdrops on them. Choose a few long sprays and curling delicate stems for balancing the design later on, and as many butterflies, bugs and bees that you are able to lay your hands on. The design is overlaid quite a lot so begin by placing the paper cutouts on the table surface, trying them in different positions until you have a balanced shape for the basis of the design. Remember to walk around the table as the picture must be attractive and balanced from each side. The larger flowers and leaves will look best forming the base of the design with smaller flowers and buds overlaid or filling in towards the top.

2 When you are satisfied, hold the design flat with the palm of your hand and chalk around the edge of the paper cutouts marking their shape on to the table surface. As the design is overlaid you will have to remove the uppermost cutouts to chalk around those underneath.

3 Turn each cutout singly face down on to the pasting board brushing on the glue evenly over the surface ensuring the edges are covered. Use a craft knife to assist in turning the cutout right side up and position on the surface within the chalk marks. As the flowers are large it is important to take great care to remove all the excess glue and air bubbles working from the centre outwards with a rolling movement of the fingers. Look at the work in an oblique light which will highlight bubbles, creases and blemishes. When the work is absolutely flat, press down the edges and wipe away excess glue with a damp sponge or kitchen paper while you are working. Continue in this fashion until the larger base flowers and leaves are in place and you can begin to build up the design. Remember **to stand back and look** every now and then as the shape and overall balance cannot be appreciated when you are right on top of it. Gaps and unevenness will appear and can be filled in with little extras cut specifically for the spaces. Keep checking that everything is pressed down flat as it really does need to be perfect on a tabletop.

4 When you are quite satisfied with the decoration, leave to dry out before cleaning up; the chalk marks will have almost disappeared but the surface of the paper and background will be gluey. With a small sponge dampened with hot water, gently remove the excess glue from the surface of the design taking care not to scuff the edges of the paper; clean the background and any remaining chalk marks. If any edges or stems pick up they can be restuck and left to dry.

### • *finishing* •

Apply an antique gold finish around the mouldings as described on page 13. Take care when painting around the top edge of the table not to stray over on to the top. Have a piece of damp kitchen roll handy to wipe any smudges off in a flash should this occur since the gold particles will be highlighted by the varnish. Leave to dry.

### • *varnishing* •

Gloss varnish is used to build up a hardwearing surface, the last 2 or 3 coats only are semi-matt. The varnishing stage is especially important in this project, and the following directions should be followed to the letter.

1 Take a takcloth and remove every particle of dust from the legs, sides, mouldings, etc, and last of all remove the dust from the tabletop working in one direction.

2 Using the clear gloss, apply a thin coat of varnish to the top, begin by brushing around the outside and filling in, spreading it on evenly to cover the entire surface. Wipe the brush on the edge of the tin to remove the

excess and, using the tip, brush over the varnished surface again working in one direction. At the first sign of drying, 'pick-up' (tackiness) or spun-sugar look, STOP! Leave to dry. Between coats, leave the brush in a jar containing white spirit: mash it about a bit and leave until the next application. You should be able to apply a coat in the morning and another in the evening or late afternoon in the right environment. Varnish drying times will vary according to room temperature but damp conditions should be avoided. At the end of each day, remove the excess varnish from the brush, mash vigorously in white spirit, wash out in soap and lukewarm water and rinse thoroughly. Leave to dry in a dust-free place. If the white spirit shows any sign of clouding throw it away.

Before each application remove all white spirit from the brush, then 'tak' to ensure all the dust has been removed from the surface of the table. Subsequent coats may be applied more generously – slurped or 'floated' on, using the same method of spreading evenly over the surface, removing the excess frequently from the brush, brushing it in one direction only, almost taking the varnish off again until it is evenly spread out. By beginning around the outside and filling in this gives you the chance to catch any runs that may spread or dribble over the moulding edge, and reduces the possibility of the edges drying or 'picking-up' before you have the chance to complete the process.

*3*   An absolute minimum of 10 coats (preferably more) must be applied before any bits of dust, hairs, etc or undulations can be removed by sanding gently with 00 grade flour paper. Do not panic when fine white scratch marks appear, these will be covered by the next layer of varnish. Keep the sandpaper away from the edges otherwise they will quickly show through. Take care not to scuff the edge or surface of the paper.

*4*   At this stage you may like to lift the table on to a working surface or tabletop to enable you to apply one or two coats to the legs and frame. Continue to apply varnish to the tabletop until the edges of the paper are no longer visible and the decoration has taken on an almost three-dimensional depth – a glow. When this stage has been reached, probably after 20 coats, you can begin the final stages of rubbing down with black 'wet and dry' 280 grade sandpaper used wet, or 0000 fine wire wool used dry (one wire-woolling might be all that is necessary). Remove dirty water with kitchen paper and wipe the surface clean. Leave to dry. Tak thoroughly before applying the next layer of varnish.

*5*   Cut off a manageable piece of wire wool and using it dry, and with *light* pressure working in a circular motion, polish up the surface until smooth. Remove *all* steel wool particles and dust. 'Tak' exceptionally thoroughly and apply another slightly thinner coat of semi-matt varnish to the surface and leave to dry for 24 hours. 'Tak' again and apply what will hopefully be the last coat of semi-matt varnish which should look as near perfect as possible. Leave to dry. Make sure the gloss varnish is entirely covered, otherwise apply another 'last' coat. Allow to harden for two or three days.

*YOU CAN ALMOST smell these sumptuous full-blown roses on a polished-slate paint-finished background*

### ◆ *polishing* ◆

Apply a generous coat of white gedgewax polish in the same direction as the grain on to the table top. Leave to dry for about 15 minutes, then buff and polish up the surface until it glows. Repeat this process several times over the next day or two and the patina will be absolutely fabulous. Stand back and admire! Your beautiful, hardwearing table will be the cause of much admiration and will give you a great deal of pleasure.

◆

# PARAVENT

*A most versatile decorative item, the little draught screen fulfils many roles; seen in the photograph as a pretty backdrop for a collection of treasured objets d'art displayed on a circular table, it looks equally attractive in a fireplace facing either way as it is decorated on both sides. Useful for concealing an ugly radiator or adding a touch of colour and interest in a corner or purely for decoration. The screen shown has panels 75cm high × 35cm wide (25 × 14 inches) and is available to order (see list of suppliers on page 143).*

## ◆ *materials list* ◆

**PARAVENT SCREEN**
**PREPARATION**
100 and 240 grade sandpaper
**PAINTING**
Small tin of white acrylic primer undercoat
250ml tin of Gardenia (or other pale colour)
   vinyl silk emulsion (for the panels)
250ml tin Slate Quarry (or similar) vinyl silk or
   matt emulsion (for the frame)
2.5cm (1 inch) brush
**DÉCOUPAGE**
4 sheets of paper depicting huge summer
   peonies, roses or other blooms of your choice
Small sharp scissors
Craft knife
Wallpaper adhesive
Glue brush
Pasting boards

Small sponge or kitchen paper
Piece of white chalk
**ANTIQUE GOLD**
Tubes of Gold and Raw Umber artists' acrylics
No. 5 artist's brush
Lidded container or jar
Water to mix ◆ Kitchen paper
**HAND-PAINTED DECORATION**
Ingredients as for the antique gold plus small tubes
   of Hooker's Green, Payne's Grey and white
   artists' acrylics
**VARNISHING**
Takcloth
Small tin of semi-matt polyurethane lacquer or
   varnish
2.5cm (1 inch) brush
Fine-grade sandpaper
White spirit

## ◆ *preparation* ◆

*1* Screens are usually constructed either from MDF (medium density fibreboard) or from a wooden frame with plywood panels, and in either case will require sanding until smooth, working in the same direction as the grain. Plywood will require more preparation and paint but the result will be worthwhile.

*2* Apply a coat of white acrylic primer undercoat and leave to dry. Sand the whole thing again and you will be surprised at the improvement in the surface, although you may have to persevere with the panels. Apply two or three more coats until you are satisfied there is a good all-over cover.

*3* Apply two or three coats of the colour you have chosen for the frame and allow to dry. Lastly paint the pale colour on the panels.

## ◆ *antique gold* ◆

Apply antique gold to the inside edge of each panel as described on page 13. The gold can also be painted on to the outside edge of the screen. Keep a piece of damp kitchen roll at the ready to whisk off any gold paint which accidentally strays on to the surface.

## ◆ *decoupage* ◆

*1* Cut a good selection of huge blooms, buds and as many leaves as possible selecting a variety of colours and

▶ *THE SUMMER peonies decorating this paravent are simple to cut*

◆

shapes. Lay the screen down flat on to a working-height surface and arrange the cutout pieces into a design over the inside panels remembering to reverse the flowers by cutting and reshaping them or altering their angle to give the panels a balanced 'mirrored' look.

*2* When you are happy with the design, hold it in place while marking around the edges of the paper with white chalk to indicate the cutouts' position when removed for pasting. As the design is overlaid, remove the uppermost pieces and mark around those below.

*3* Turn each cutout singly face down on to the pasting board and brush on the glue evenly taking it out over the edges. Turn upright and place in position on the panel, working the excess glue and air from the middle outwards with a rolling finger movement. When every blemish is removed and the cutout is flat, press the edges down. Continue in the same way until you are happy with the picture. **Stand back and look** occasionally; if it is possible to position the screen in an oblique light,

it will show up any air bubbles or little creases. Excess glue can be cleaned off as you work with dampened kitchen roll.

*4* Leave the design to dry out thoroughly before taking a small sponge or kitchen paper to clean both the background and surface of the paper.

*5* It is a matter of personal taste whether you wish to decorate the outside panels in the same fashion, or with a small posy of flowers in one corner, each corner, or for the flowers to cascade from the top as I have done. Follow the guidelines previously given.

### • *finishing* •

If desired, brighten up the frame by hand-painting a twisted ribbon and bows and leaves as described on page 22. Leave to dry, then varnish as described on pages 13–14. Varnish the inner panels first (the frame can be given a couple of coats at the end), and brush the varnish in one direction (top to bottom).

PEONIES CASCADE *from the top of the screen and hand-painted ribbons and leaves add interest to the frame*

# FIRESCREEN

*This firescreen or fireboard turned out to be an absolutely stunning piece of work. The wonderful hollyhocks in full bloom positively glow against the dark background which shows them up in their full splendour. Smaller, darker flowers are scattered on the dark paint-finish, some actually merge into it giving the whole picture dimension and depth. The firescreen measures 80cm high × 57cm wide (32 × 23 inches) and is constructed from plywood in a pine frame, standing on two feet. Similar screens are available to order (see suppliers on page 143).*

---

## • materials list •

**FIRESCREEN**
**PREPARATION**
100 and 240 grade sandpaper
**PAINTING**
Small tin of white acrylic primer undercoat
250ml tin of black vinyl matt emulsion
2.5cm (1 inch) brush
Small natural sea-sponge
250ml tins of light- to mid-blue and Raw
   Umber vinyl matt emulsion **or** large tubes of
   artists' acrylics in the same colours
2 lidded containers
Small tin of Unibond/PVA
Old spoon for measuring
Water to mix
**DÉCOUPAGE**
3 sheets of good quality wrapping paper
Small sharp scissors

Craft knife
Wallpaper adhesive
Small glue brush
Pasting boards
Small sponge or kitchen paper
Piece of white chalk
**ANTIQUE GOLD**
Small tubes of Gold and Raw Umber artists'
   acrylics
No. 4 artist's brush
Lidded container or jar
Water to mix
**VARNISHING**
Takcloth
Small tin of semi-matt or pale eggshell varnish
   or polyurethane lacquer
2.5cm (1 inch) brush
Fine-grade sandpaper  •  White spirit

---

◆

## ◆ *preparation* ◆

*1* Rub the whole screen down using 100 grade sandpaper working in the same direction as the grain in the wood.

*2* Apply a coat of acrylic primer undercoat and when this is dry, sand the screen down again. Apply two more coats of acrylic primer undercoat and when dry, sand all the surfaces with fine sandpaper until the finish feels good to the touch.

*3* Apply two or three coats of black emulsion paint to both sides of the screen including the frame, legs and feet.

*4* Measure out one tablespoon of blue emulsion and the same amount of Unibond with up to four tablespoons of water. Mix the glaze. In a second container mix a small quantity of Raw Umber emulsion glaze as above. Try to approach this work as if it were a painting or a work of art (which it is after all!). There should be great depth in the background to enable the flowers of a similar colour to merge into it while the huge pale blooms of the hollyhocks catch the light in the foreground.

*5* Paint the top half of the board blue, the bottom half black, going over it until the colour is strong. To avoid a straight join line where the colours meet, use the tip of the brush, 'streak' it to merge the colours and make the brush marks obvious. Sponge on Raw Umber to get some depth into the picture. The brush can be dipped (without cleaning) into the umber and streaked across the blue leaving patches of blue showing through. Apply both the colours with a sponge leaving the spongemarks to add interest; the base of the panel should be dark. Let the sponging go over on to the frame so that the finish is broken.

## ◆ *découpage* ◆

*1* Lay the panel on to a working height surface with the legs sticking out in front. If you are able to get hold of this wonderful hollyhock paper (Huijsum Hollyhocks by National Gallery, No. 300133) you will see it has everything to offer in light and shade, and the background is similar in colour to the screen. The huge white flowers have been reshaped and the tall centre stem elongated and another bud or two added to balance the overall picture. The pale green buds and leaves catch the light and the flowers appear to grow from the base of the screen.

Cut out several large blooms and a lot of leaves, the selection is limited and you must improvise: by reshaping the same leaves and by using them at different angles they will appear more varied. The long central stem is elongated to twice its original length by cutting two and carefully overlaying one on to the other so that no join is discernible. This stem and the largest blooms were stuck down first and the remainder added around them. I hope you will enjoy doing it as much as I did.

*2* When you have cut a good selection of flowers, etc lay the long central stem on to the panel and add the large blooms around the base. Check that it is centred and chalk around it leaving the shape on the background; this will be a tremendous help when you have to remove the pieces for pasting. Add leaves and buds, building up the design; mark it out again.

*3* Turn each cutout singly face down on to the pasting board and brush on the glue evenly over the surface taking the brush out over the edges of the paper. A craft knife is useful to lift the cutouts off the board. Turn right side up and position on the screen. Press any excess glue and air bubbles out, working from the centre of each bloom outwards with a rolling finger movement, and wipe away with damp kitchen roll. When every blemish has been removed and the surface is flat, press down the edges. Try the flowers and leaves in their positions, building up the design and filling in gaps as you go along. Think whether they need to be overlaid or their stems tucked under a flower and so on. **Stand back and look** occasionally. Last of all add the dark blooms placing them in different positions until you are happy with the design. Leave to dry.

*4* Remove all traces of glue from the surface of the paper and the background using a damp sponge or kitchen paper. Leave to dry.

## ◆ *finishing* ◆

Apply an antique gold finish to the inside edge of the frame with the utmost care as described on page 13. Have some dampened kitchen roll by you to whisk off any gold that accidentally strays on to the picture. Leave to dry, then varnish as described on pages 13–14. Apply the first coat of varnish sparingly – this is important otherwise the white blooms will absorb the varnish and lose their vibrance and beauty. Apply sufficient layers to lose the edges of the paper and the 'stuck on' look. The more you apply the greater dimension and depth the picture will have. Stand back and admire!

▶ *HUGE HOLLYHOCKS glow against the dark background of this firescreen*

◆

# THREE-FOLD SCREEN

*The design on this lavishly decorated screen is applied to a strong red background using a paper which is taken from a print of a French tapestry circa 1490, entitled 'The Lady and the Unicorn' and published by Caspari. The paper is very beautiful in its own right and it seems dreadful to dissect it in such a way, but the colours were perfect for the effect I was trying to achieve!*
*The magnificent heavenly angels which emerge from the background are taken from a Christmas paper 'Adoration of the Angels' published by Alan Hutchison Ltd. Parts of the patchwork have been elaborately decorated with gilded scrolls and the 'carved' frame is created from hand-coloured photocopies of Renaissance carving which has been richly gilded in liquid gold-leaf. Extravagant cords and tassels from Laura Ashley add the finishing touch to this sumptuous project. Screens are available by mail order (see suppliers list on page 143). The inner panels of the screen illustrated measure 156cm × 42cm (62 × 17 inches).*

## ◆ *materials list* ◆

**THREE-FOLD SCREEN**
**PREPARATION**
100 grit sandpaper or glasspaper
240 grit glasspaper or flour paper
**PAINTING**
Tin of white acrylic primer undercoat
Small tin of tomato-red vinyl matt emulsion (or
 any colour of your choice)
2 × 2.5cm (1 inch) brushes
**DÉCOUPAGE**
Up to 8 sheets of colourful background paper
 for the patchwork
6 sheets of 'Adoration of the Angels' or a
 similar Christmas paper
2 sheets of smaller angel paper, or any similar
 contrasting paper of your choice
Small sharp scissors
Craft knife
Wallpaper adhesive
Glue brush

At least two pasting boards, preferably more
Small sponge and kitchen paper
Container of water
Piece of white chalk
**HAND-PAINTED DECORATION**
Small tin of dark- or mid-brown emulsion
Small bottle of liquid gold leaf (spirit-based)
No. 5 artist's brush
**VARNISHING**
Takcloth
Litre tin of semi-matt polyurethane lacquer or
 pale craft varnish
2.5cm (1 inch) brush
Fine-grade sandpaper
White spirit
**OPTIONAL**
If your screen is constructed of plywood you may
 need to mix an emulsion glaze and will therefore
 need a tin of Unibond/PVA adhesive and a lidded
 jar or container.

## ◆ *preparation* ◆

Work on each panel separately and hinge them together when the work is completed.

**If your screen is made from plywood** it is important to spend time on the preparation as it has a tell-tale straight 'grain' and can have very rough splintery patches. When painting or sanding down *always* work in the same direction as the grain.

*1* Use a sheet of 100 grit sandpaper to rub down the frame thoroughly. A coat of sanding sealer may be

applied to a new frame and knots in softwood should be treated with knotting. *Do not sand the panels at this stage.*

*2* Apply the first coat of acrylic primer undercoat. Paint the frame as well as the inner panels. Leave to dry. This will strengthen any loose splintery areas of ply thereby making sanding possible.

▶ *MAGNIFICENT ANGELS emerge from a lavish patchwork of colour — all cut from wrapping paper*

*3* Using 100 grit sandpaper sand the whole thing down, again paying particular attention to the worst patches. If the patchiness and roughness cannot be eradicated (which is quite usual), mix an emulsion glaze using equal parts of matt emulsion and Unibond/PVA adhesive mixed with up to four parts of water. Use the vinyl matt emulsion in the colour you have chosen for the screen's topcoat.

*4* Apply the glaze to the screen and frame and allow to dry. Apply another two coats and you will find that the surface has improved dramatically.

**If your screen is made from medium density fibreboard (MDF)**

*1* Apply the first coat of acrylic primer undercoat and leave to dry.

*2* Use a sheet of 100 grit sandpaper and sand down the whole thing, until it feels smooth to the touch, especially the edges. Remember to sand in one direction only.

*3* Dust off and apply another three coats of primer undercoat allowing to dry between coats and sanding down any build-up of paint on the edges as you go along, using the finer sandpaper.

*4* Apply two or three coats of the colour you have chosen for the screen's topcoat.

### ◆ *the frame* ◆

Paint and decorate the frame first, then there will be no likelihood of splashing paint on to your découpage design!

*1* The simplest method is to paint the frame a brown wood colour and when it is dry, to paint bold scrolls and squiggles to represent carving.

*2* An alternative is to use photocopies of wood carving printed on sheets of paper. Photocopies of wood carving and ornamental scrolls are available from Dover Inc (see suppliers list on page 142) in a book entitled *Ornamental Borders, Scrolls and Cartouches*. (Yet another option is to stain the frame in a wood colour of your choice or to paint it in antique gold – see page 13.) Begin by painting all the sheets of paper with watered-down brown emulsion paint – the paint you used for the frame will do – which will allow the detail to show through. Allow to dry out, then cut out the painted carvings, paste the back of each strip singly and apply to the frame, butting the edges of the next strip to it. Stick the photocopies on all three panels and allow to dry out.

Colour in the carving using the brown paint in normal strength, omitting the uppermost pieces which you will highlight next with liquid gold leaf. Allow to dry, then with an artist's brush highlight the remaining carving with liquid gold leaf. **Stand back occasionally** to observe your work from a distance. Paint around the inside edge of the frame and don't worry if you stray a little on to the panel – it will be covered later by the découpage design.

*3* Paint the outside edge of the frame in antique gold acrylics, see page 13. Allow the whole thing to dry.

### ◆ *découpage* ◆

You will find it much easier to work if the panel is laid on a flat surface such as a tabletop. Alternatively the three sections can be placed against a wall or on the floor, but the latter may cause you some discomfort as you will have to kneel down for long periods.

*1* Begin by cutting the colourful background paper into different shapes, dissecting the different colours separately. Make up your own patchwork for the background; concentrate on cutting a good number of shapes in as wide a variety as possible. The patterns can be used in any direction to provide more interest, but any animals look decidedly better on their feet!

The paper cutouts have to be juggled about rather like a jigsaw puzzle to fill in the gaps, turning them this way and that. Cut triangles, squares, rectangles and ovals, in fact any shape at all, to utilize every tiny piece of pattern and colour on a sheet.

*2* **First outside panel** Begin by laying the pieces of cutout paper on the top of the first panel fitting them into the top corners. At the same time, cut out the first row of angels selecting the three on the top row of the screen. Lay them down on the panel to see whether they fit into the space or if they need to be trimmed. The patchwork should completely surround the angels, being large enough to fit slightly underneath them. If it is helpful, chalk around the shapes, marking their outline on to the coloured panel, otherwise fit them in as you go along.

Turn each cutout singly face down on to the pasting board and brush the glue evenly over the surface taking the brush out over the edges of the paper. A craft knife is useful to lift the cutouts from the board. Turn right side up and position on the panel, pressing out any excess glue and air bubbles and wiping away with damp kitchen paper.

*3* Fit the angels into position again, if they cover the background of patchwork, chalk around them. If not, paste on more background shapes to fill any gaps. Paste angels and place within the chalk marks. Press down from the middle outwards leaving the edges loose until all the air and glue has been worked out to the edges, then press the edges down.

From the top of the panel to the bottom of the first block of angels (two rows) measures 53cm (21 inches – see below). Cut out and paste another section of patchwork about 21cm (8½ inches) deep before the next block of angels. Repeat the same procedure each time.

4 If you are using the same paper as me alterations will have to be made to the last row of angels as they are too wide to fit the panel. Do try to dissect and reshape them logically; this is not nearly as complicated as it sounds as the cutting is simple and straightforward. The main thing is always to lay the paper shapes on to the panel to see what they look like and how they fit, and make the necessary alterations before continuing.

5 **Second outside panel** Repeat steps 2 to 4. It is vital that the two outer panels should be the same and now is the time to stand them upright alongside one another to either measure or mark out the design. The height at which the rows of angels start must coincide as their halos are very noticeable!

6 **Middle panel** Repeat steps 2 to 4. I have used a different paper with a smaller motif on this panel, introducing the larger angels at the base to tie the overall design together.

### ◆ scroll work (optional) ◆

Paint sheets of scrolls with watered down brown matt emulsion paint (as you did with the 'carving' for the frame). Allow to dry out. Paste and apply to the panels wherever you think best, especially if there are ugly edges within the découpage that would benefit from being covered up! Allow all three panels to dry out thoroughly. Clean the surfaces carefully with a damp sponge or kitchen roll.

### ◆ varnishing ◆

Place all three panels in an upright position. Tak off any dust from the frames and panels. Apply the first coat of varnish sparingly and allow to dry. Apply approximately 10 coats of varnish to the inside panels, takking each beforehand and allowing to dry thoroughly between each coat. The frames will require about four coats of varnish. When the panels are quite dry, attach the hinges and you will have an exceptionally sturdy piece of furniture and one which, I am sure, will look absolutely superb. Well done!

53 cm
(21 in)

*THE HEIGHT at which the rows of angels start on the outside panels should coincide as their haloes are very noticeable*

# 8

# THE BEDROOM

The character of our bedroom may change over the years, but it should always be a sanctuary, a very personal and private place – not always possible if there are small children in the house! It should have a romantic feel, be functional yet cosy in the colder months, comfortable and quiet for rest and sleep, fresh and airy when the windows are flung wide in fine weather to allow sunlight, breeze and birdsong to filter in.

Make a rose garland for your bedside table, pretty up your dressing-table with a pair of candlestick lamps or a fabulous dressing-table set, or for a really romantic touch try decorating an enchanting floral headboard.

♦ ♦ ♦ ♦

## FLORAL HEADBOARD

*The headboard is made from MDF (medium density fibreboard) of the best quality and is available in different shapes (see list of suppliers on page 143).*

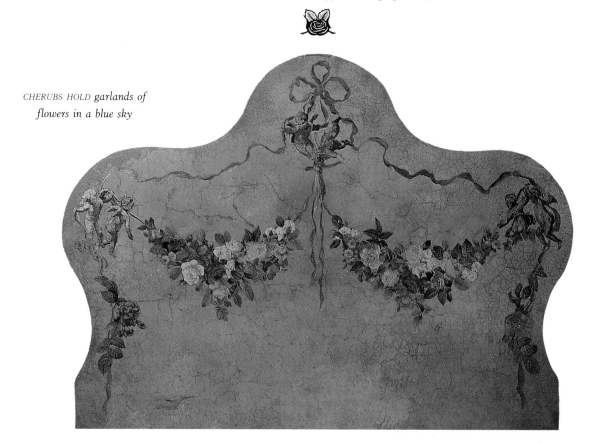

*CHERUBS HOLD garlands of flowers in a blue sky*

## • materials list •

**MDF HEADBOARD**
**PREPARATION**
100 and 240 grade sandpaper
**PAINTING**
Small tin of white acrylic primer undercoat
2.5cm (1 inch) brush
250ml tins of mid-blue and pale turquoise blue
  emulsion
Small amount of yellow acrylic or emulsion to
  add sunlight (optional)
White primer undercoat used previously
Small tin of Unibond/PVA
Lidded container
Natural sea-sponge   •   Water to mix
**DÉCOUPAGE**
6 sheets of good quality wrapping paper (these
  can be mixed as long as they are of the same
  thickness) illustrated with roses
A sheet of paper with cherubs
Small sharp scissors   •   Craft knife
Wallpaper adhesive
Glue brush   •   Pasting boards
Small sponge or kitchen paper
Piece of white chalk
**ANTIQUE GOLD**
Tubes of Gold and Raw Umber artists' acrylics
No. 4 artist's brush
Lidded container or jar
Water to mix
**CRAQUELURE**
Materials as listed on page 25

## • preparation •

1   Rub down the edges of the headboard with 100 grade sandpaper; remove dust and paint both sides of the headboard with white primer undercoat. Leave to dry. Rub down the edges with 240 grade sandpaper, feel it with your fingers to ensure it is smooth. Apply two more coats of primer undercoat, letting it dry between coats.
2   Paint on two coats of mid-blue emulsion to both sides and allow to dry. For the 'right' side mix the emulsion glaze by combining one tablespoon of pale turquoise blue, one tablespoon of Unibond/PVA adhesive and approximately three tablespoons of water. The aim is to produce a sky-like effect (see page 19 for sponging techniques). Sponge on the pale turquoise

colour in places. Dip the sponge as it is into the darker colour and sponge on in patches. Sponge white on especially at the top of the headboard. Leave to dry for a while before softly sponging on some more white for cottonwool clouds. Leave to dry.

## • découpage •

1   Make two or three chalk marks at different points to indicate the centre of the headboard. Chalk a floppy bow at the top, mark the positions of the three groups of cherubs on the headboard, cut them out and paste on first. Draw the ribbons and outline the swags in chalk (they can be erased several times until you get them right). See pages 22–5 for hand-painted finishing touches.
2   Cut a good selection of roses, leaves, etc and place them on the headboard to form a pleasing design. When you are satisfied with it, chalk round the outline.
3   Place the cutouts singly face down on the pasting board and brush the glue evenly over the surface ensuring the edges are covered. Turn right side up with a craft knife if it is helpful, and position on the headboard. Work out any air bubbles, blemishes and excess glue with your fingers wiping it away carefully with damp kitchen paper. This is an overlaid design that can be built up gradually sticking on a few of the choicest blooms in the uppermost positions, particularly those which will catch the light. Leaves are very important to add depth to the work and for a natural look.
   When the cutouts are flat press the edges of each one down as you proceed. When the decoration is finished leave it to dry. **Stand back and look** and if any gaps require filling in do so now. When the surface is dry the work can be cleaned up with a damp sponge or kitchen paper. Leave to dry.

## • hand-painted decoration •

Paint the gold ribbons and bow as described on page 22 using antique gold (see page 13). Shade the ribbons well using raw umber on the same brush as the gold, painting the ribbon to join up with the découpage swags to complete the picture. Leave to dry.

## • finishing •

Apply a single coat of semi-matt varnish to protect the découpage. Leave to dry, then apply an antique craquelure finish (see page 26) followed by 2 coats of semi-matt varnish. When the headboard is completely dry, polish with gedgewax as described on page 83.

# CANDLESTICK LAMPS

*Here is something really special for your bedroom. Take time to think about a design and colour that will complement your décor. Use tiny forget-me-nots or rosebuds, blossom or tiny humming birds with miniature pink blossom for an oriental feel; twist and twine leaves and flowers down the stem with a hand-painted ribbon, and gild the mouldings as a finishing touch.*
*The candlesticks can be sponge-finished first in a delicate shade (see page 19) or simply painted in emulsion. Look in the list of suppliers on page 143 for faux candles, brass followers, electrified or liquid candles and the candlesticks themselves. The shades are also available – why not découpage the shade too?*

## • *materials list* •

**PAIR OF WOODEN CANDLESTICKS**
 approximately 20–25cm (8–10 inches) high
**PREPARATION**
240 grade sandpaper
**PAINTING**
Small tin of white acrylic primer undercoat
Small brush
250ml tin of cream (or colour of your choice)
 vinyl matt or silk emulsion
**DÉCOUPAGE**
Good quality wrapping paper illustrated with
 tiny rosebuds or other delicate motifs
Small sharp scissors
Craft knife
Wallpaper paste
Glue brush
Pasting board
Small sponge or kitchen paper
**ANTIQUE GOLD**
Small tubes of Gold and Raw Umber artists'
 acrylics
No. 4 artist's brush
Lidded container or jar
Water to mix
**VARNISHING**
Takcloth
Small tin of semi-matt pale varnish or
 polyurethane lacquer
Small brush
Fine-grade sandpaper
White spirit
**ACCESSORIES**
2 brass followers and 2 candleshades of your
 choice (see list of suppliers on page 143)

◄ *CANDLESHADES and candles echo the deep pink of the
rosebuds on the candlesticks*

## • *preparation* •

1  If necessary, rub down the candlesticks with sand-paper checking the rim and base edges are smooth.
2  Apply at least two coats of acrylic primer undercoat allowing it to dry between coats.
3  Apply two coats of cream emulsion, turning the candlestick upside down to check that all the surface is covered. Leave to dry.

## • *découpage* •

The candlesticks can be decorated in a number of ways; have a look at porcelain candlesticks in antique shops to get some good ideas. Tiny rosebuds, birds, ribbons, trailing ivy leaves or honeysuckle can look lovely on the stem with a few larger blooms on the base. The choice is yours!
1  Cut out with great care as intricate flowers and stems will look unattractive with the background showing. If the stems are long, fine and curling, cut them into sections and butt them together when they are pasted and applied to the surface, the joins will not show if they are done accurately.
2  Turn each paper cutout face down on to the pasting board and apply the glue evenly over the surface taking it out over the edges onto the board to ensure that the edges have glue on them. Lift from the board using a craft knife, turn right side up and paste to the candle-stick. Press out excess glue and air bubbles with your fingers, wiping it away with damp kitchen paper. When the surface of the paper is flat, press down the edges.
3  When the decoration is complete leave to dry before cleaning up the surface of the paper and background with a damp sponge or kitchen paper.

## • *finishing* •

Apply an antique gold finish to the mouldings working as described on page 13. Allow to dry, then varnish as described on pages 13–14 taking care that the varnish doesn't gather and run on the mouldings. Five coats will probably suffice.

# DRESSING-TABLE SET

*In most homes it is not uncommon to find one or two old items which have become scratched, faded or worn. These may be tin, enamel, plastic or wood. The oval tin tray fell into this category and was perfect for transformation. The hand mirror was discoloured white plastic which looked most unattractive but nevertheless had a pleasing shape. An old hairbrush of a similar shape could perhaps be sought out to complete the set.*

---

## • materials list •

### METAL TRAY AND PLASTIC MIRROR

**PREPARATION**

Red oxide primer

Small tin of matt varnish (or small shellac
   varnish thinned with methylated spirit)

2 × 2.5cm (1 inch) brushes

White spirit

Kitchen paper

**PAINTING**

White acrylic undercoat

Small tins of cream and white vinyl silk
   emulsion

Small brush

Lidded container or jar

Small natural sea-sponge

Water to mix

**DÉCOUPAGE**

Paper covered in the tiniest roses and other
   pretty flowers, buds and leaves

Small sharp scissors

Craft knife

Wallpaper paste

Glue brush   •   Pasting board

Small sponge or kitchen paper

Piece of white chalk

**ANTIQUE GOLD**

Small tubes of Gold and Raw Umber artists'
   acrylics

No. 4 artist's brush

Lidded container or jar

Water to mix

**VARNISHING**

Takcloth

Small tin of semi-matt pale craft varnish of
   polyurethane lacquer

2.5cm (1 inch) brush

## • decorating the tray •

*1* Prepare the tray as described on pages 15–18. When
the red oxide primer is completely dry apply white
acrylic undercoat followed by two or three coats of white
vinyl silk emulsion.

*2* Apply a simple sponged-on paint finish (see page 19)

◄ *A PLASTIC mirror and tin tray completely transformed: this
delightful pair would grace any dressing-table*

using cream vinyl silk lightly sponged over the surface
at random. Dip the tip of the sponge directly into the tin
and keep sponging all over the surface until it looks even
but with the white still visible.

*3* Chalk a vague diamond shape on to the surface of the
tray and stick on one or two flowers to mark out the
shape. From this rough guide the rest of the flowers and
leaves are stuck on rather like a jigsaw puzzle – wherever
their shape looks as if it will fit. Many of the flowers
shown are overlapped by others, and leaves and buds
have been tucked into gaps.

Place each cutout singly face down on to the pasting
board and apply the paste ensuring that the edges are
covered. Lift with a craft knife and position on the tray.
This is called an overlaid design. Although quite time
consuming, it is relatively easy as there is no set pattern
or design; the flowers and leaves are stuck in every
direction but it is useful to keep turning the tray round
to check that the shape looks balanced from all angles.
If the overall shape is slightly off-centre, the hand-
painted ribbons (see below) will even the whole thing
out.

*4* When completely dry clean the work to remove
excess glue from the surface using damp kitchen paper
or a small sponge.

*5* Apply an antique gold finish to the outside rim of the
tray as described on page 13. Then add some twisted
ribbons and bows or other decoration of your choice
using the techniques described on pages 22–5. Finally,
varnish as described on pages 13–14.

## • decorating the hand mirror •

*1* Paint the mirror back and frame with two coats of
matt varnish or shellac, allowing to dry between coats.
Apply two coats of white undercoat, again allowing to
dry, followed by two coats of white vinyl silk. Be careful
not to smudge paint on to the mirror glass.

*2* Apply a cream sponge finish as before.

*3* Use the leftover paper from the tray to decorate the
hand mirror. There is no need to chalk a shape this time,
simply follow the shape of the mirror, sticking on the
flowers facing in different directions. Start from the
middle so that the flowers around the outside show up
clearly above the others, so giving the design depth.
Allow to dry.

*4* After cleaning the excess glue from the surface of the
work, paint a bow and a broken ribbon through the
flowers ending with two trailing ribbons on the handle.
Allow to dry, then varnish as before.

# 9
# THE GUESTROOM

*P*retty bed-linen, scented herb sachets for the drawers, fresh flowers, magazines and books, fresh fruit and cordials all help to provide a welcome when friends are coming to stay. Smarten up an old chest of drawers with a paint-finish, or découpage a mirror or photograph frame. Perhaps you have a lovely big tray to decorate on which your guests could enjoy early morning tea or breakfast in bed.

• • • •

# OCTAGONAL MIRROR

*I bought this old frame for next to nothing. As you can see from the photograph it has been transformed by painting it a gorgeous shade of turquoise blue with a simple design of single, hand-painted roses taken from an eighteenth-century textile print. The roses are 'tied' together with a twisted ribbon painted in acrylics.*

## • materials list •

**MIRROR FRAME**
**PREPARATION**
Small tin of matt varnish (or shellac varnish
   thinned with methylated spirit)
2.5cm (1 inch) brush
**PAINTING**
Small white primer undercoat
Sample pot of turquoise emulsion
Small brush
**DÉCOUPAGE**
Wrapping paper with a rose design
Small sharp scissors
Craft knife
Wallpaper adhesive
Small glue brush

Pasting board • Small sponge or kitchen paper
**ANTIQUE GOLD**
Tubes of Gold and Raw Umber artists' acrylics
No. 4 artist's brush
Lidded container or jar
Water to mix
**VARNISHING**
Takcloth
Small tin of semi-matt varnish or polyurethane
   lacquer
2.5cm (1 inch) brush
White spirit
**Mirror glass** can be ordered and cut to your
requirements at hardware stores, decorating shops
and some DIY stores

## • preparation •

1  Paint the frame with two coats of matt varnish or shellac to seal it and stop the dark stain seeping into the paint. Let it dry between coats.
2  Apply two coats of white undercoat and let it dry, then at least two coats of the turquoise emulsion. Allow to dry.

## • découpage •

1  This is a simple design using only the rose blooms, cut out as many as you require.
2  Turn each cutout face down on the pasting board and

apply the glue evenly all over; turn right side up using a craft knife and apply to the frame, working the air and glue out with your fingers until the surface is flat then press down the edges. Let it dry.
3  When the work is completely dry, clean up the surface with a damp sponge or kitchen paper.

## • finishing •

Decorate in antique gold (page 13), painting ribbons and bows, etc as described on pages 22–5. Leave to dry, then varnish as described on pages 13–14.

◄ ROSES AND RIBBONS *adorn an octagonal mirror*

# PARCHMENT CHEST OF DRAWERS

*A Victorian pine chest of drawers of inferior quality, 'grained' to cover its shortcomings, and probably built originally for servants' quarters, has been transformed by a charming parchment finish, hand-painted with swags of leaves and berries, and aged and craquelured.*
*The paint-finish is all applied with a sponge; the swags of leaves and berries are hand-painted and easy to master after a little initial practice on paper. Even without decoration it would be attractive in this lovely ochre colour which works well with most colour schemes.*

### ◆ *materials list* ◆

**WOODEN CHEST OF DRAWERS**
**PREPARATION**
100 grade sandpaper or glasspaper
240 grade flour paper or glasspaper
If your furniture has been stained in a dark colour
   you will also need a small tin of matt varnish
   (or shellac varnish thinned with methylated
   spirit) and an old brush
**PAINTING**
Small tin of white acrylic primer undercoat
Small tin of Gardenia or other pale cream vinyl
   silk emulsion paint
Small tubes of Yellow Ochre, White, Raw
Umber or Payne's Grey artists' acrylics

2.5cm (1 inch) brush
Small tin of Unibond/PVA adhesive
Lidded container or carton
Small natural sea-sponge
Water to mix
**HAND-PAINTED DECORATION**
Small tubes of Hooker's Green and Venetian
   Red artists' acrylics
Payne's Grey and white as above
No. 4 artist's brush
A piece of white chalk
Kitchen paper
**CRAQUELURE**
Materials as listed on page 25

▶ *A PRETTY CHEST of drawers which would fit into almost any colour scheme*

### ◆ *preparation – painted item* ◆

Remove the handles and the drawers from the frame. With 100 grade sandpaper, rub down the chest and drawers working always in the same direction as the grain in the wood if you can see it.

Rub through the paint on the edges of drawers, top, locks, escutcheons, etc. This will provide a 'key' on which to paint.
(*NOTE*   If the chest has many layers of paint which have become uneven, blistered or unsightly it may be better to use a professional paint stripping or pine stripping service who usually collect and deliver. If you have a lot of time and patience, you can use a proprietary paint stripper.)

### ◆ *preparation – dark stained wood* ◆

If the chest is stained it will discolour the paint, and to avoid this a barrier has to be formed between the two. Rub down as above with 100 grade sandpaper, remove dust and paint the chest with either a coat of matt varnish or two coats of shellac varnish thinned a little with methylated spirit (allow shellac 30 minutes between coats). Let it dry.

### ◆ *painting* ◆

*1*   Apply a coat of white primer undercoat and let it dry. Run your fingers over the chest and the drawers and smooth out any rough patches with 240 grade sand- or glasspaper. Apply at least another two coats of acrylic

DETAIL OF *a craquelure finish*

*CHALK THE OUTLINE of your chosen shape onto the top of the chest. Paint the stem and leaves, returning to shade them, filling in with berries to balance the design*

primer undercoat allowing it to dry between coats. Check drawer edges for build-up of paint which may affect their closing and remove with sandpaper if necessary.

2   Apply two coats of vinyl silk emulsion in Gardenia or another pale cream and let it dry.

3   Mix an emulsion glaze using equal parts of white emulsion and Unibond (two tablespoons of each will be enough) mixed with 1–4 parts water. Using the container's lid as a palette, squeeze out about an inch of Yellow Ochre tube paint, a spoonful of pale cream and a tiny blob of Raw Umber or Payne's Grey. These will have to be replenished as you go along. Have a spoonful of white emulsion on the lid if there is room.

4   Apply the sponged paint-finish. Start with the sides to get the hang of it before tackling the front. Replace the drawers so that the paint-finish can cover the whole surface and the lines can flow. You can ease the drawers out a little using a screwdriver in their keyholes when you have finished to avoid sticking. Squeeze the sponge out in water, removing any excess on kitchen paper. Dip a little of the sponge in the glaze then into the yellow ochre. Work from a top corner sponging diagonally; dip the sponge into two colours at once and cover the surface with some basic markings to give it movement and

shape, filling in other areas with a paler colour. The desired effect is illustrated on page 20.

5   Leave to dry before building up the paint further. Anything you dislike can be whited out and altered. Introduce a thin vein of Payne's Grey or patches of Raw Umber to add depth and interest. Wash the sponge several times while you are working as it becomes impossible to differentiate between the colours. It is a matter of choice whether the colour is vibrant or delicate; colours can be intensified, but the overall effect of a subdued parchment finish is a lovely glow of soft yellow and you will find that it fits into many different room schemes.

### ◆ *hand-painted leaves and berries* ◆

Using the keyhole as a guide make a vertical chalk mark in the centre of each drawer and an inch in from either edge, and join together with a deep curve. This may take several attempts – wipe away mistakes until all the curves look the same. Decorate using the techniques described on pages 22–3.

### ◆ *finishing* ◆

Apply an antique craquelure finish (see page 26) and polish as described on page 83.

# ROSE GARLAND TABLE

ROSE GARLAND TABLE *It is very easy to find a small occasional table in a second-hand shop or flea market; you may even have one in your home which can be transformed. This old mahogany table was first stripped and then painted with several coats of black vinyl matt emulsion. It is a good idea to turn the table upside down on to a working-height surface to apply the first coat of emulsion; when it is dry, turn the table upright and paint everywhere else. Leave to dry and apply further coats until you are satisfied with the coverage.*

*The découpage design was easily cut from a sheet of good quality wrapping paper covered in roses. As the tabletop is octagonal a garland of flowers arranged in a rough circle looks rather pretty with a central posy on the tray base. The table was very pitted and uneven but the surface has been greatly improved by the application of many layers of varnish. The entire project cost very little and the result is a most attractive bedside table. Polish occasionally with clear wax polish to give it a lovely patina and depth.*

# BREAKFAST TRAY

*LARGE BREAKFAST TRAY* Perfect for treating your guests to
breakfast in bed the next time they visit. Paint-finished with
the leftovers from the parchment chest of drawers, and
decorated in a wonderful paper illustrating antique roses, lilies
and convolvulus which was used on the Edwardian jug and fat
coffee pot (pages 38 and 32), and, with other papers, on the
commode (page 69).

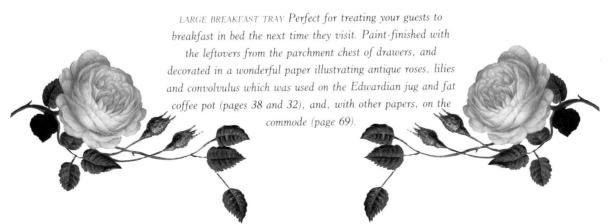

# *10*

# THE BATHROOM AND
# DRESSING-ROOM

*B*athrooms can be so boring. Those in modern houses often have little or no natural light and are tiled from floor to ceiling, making them practical but sterile places. A piece of furniture can transform a bathroom. A small chest, cupboard, dressing-table or washstand is well suited to this room; add a few pictures on the walls and some fresh flowers to bring life and comfort to an otherwise dull and purely functional area. The projects shown would adorn a dressing-room equally effectively.

◆　◆　◆　◆

*A BLUE SPONGED finish on a white background has brought this shabby washstand to life*

◆

# VICTORIAN WASHSTAND

*Simple sponging and delicately coloured flowers cut from congratulations paper and formed into bunches have transformed a shabby washstand into a charming piece of furniture which would make an eye-catching focal point in a bathroom or dressing-room.*

*When I stripped the paint from this probably home-made washstand I found burn marks, immovable black ink stains on the top surface and an unsightly jumble of ill-matched wood. One of the back legs had been replaced owing to woodworm.*

*The washstand shown measures 72 × 60 × 39cm (29 × 24 × 16 inches) and has been painted with white vinyl silk emulsion and simply and quickly sponged with a blue fast-drying emulsion glaze before applying the découpage decoration.*

*The pretty little jug, bowl, mug and chamberpot were collected from different sources over a period of time and made into a set using matching decoration.*

## • materials list •

**WASHSTAND**

**PREPARATION**

100 grade sandpaper

Small tin of matt varnish or shellac varnish
   thinned with methylated spirit (if your
   furniture has been stained a dark colour)

2.5cm (1 inch) brush

**PAINTING**

Small tin of white primer/undercoat

Small tin of white vinyl silk emulsion

Sample pot of pale to mid-blue emulsion

Small Unibond/PVA adhesive

2.5cm (1 inch) brush

Natural sea-sponge

Old spoon for measuring

Lidded container or jar

Water to mix

**DÉCOUPAGE**

3 sheets of pretty wrapping paper, preferably
   illustrated with stemmed flowers

Small sharp scissors

Craft knife  •  Wallpaper paste

Glue brush  •  Pasting board

Small sponge or kitchen paper

**VARNISHING**

Takcloth

250ml tin of pale eggshell or semi-matt varnish
   or polyurethane lacquer

2.5cm (1 inch) brush

White spirit

## • preparation •

*1a* If your washstand is already painted, rub it down thoroughly with 100 grade sandpaper to provide a 'key' on which to paint.

*1b* If it is stained a dark colour paint it with matt varnish or shellac to seal it and prevent the stain marking the paint. Let it dry.

*1c* For a stripped pine washstand as this was, sand with 100 grade sandpaper in the direction of the woodgrain, paying particular attention to edges.

*2* Remove all dust. Apply the first coat of primer/undercoat and let it dry. Rub down again. Apply at least two more undercoats allowing the paint to dry between each coat. Then apply two coats of white vinyl silk, again allowing to dry between coats.

*3* Mix an emulsion glaze of two tablespoons of blue emulsion, the same of Unibond and one to four table-spoons of water.

Rinse sponge in cold water and remove excess moisture on kitchen paper. Dip the sponge into the emulsion glaze and squeeze it out. Using a light wrist movement sponge the glaze all over the washstand. It is fast drying and the sponge will need replenishing frequently. Leave areas you plan to decorate lighter. Leave to dry.

## • découpage •

*1* Cut out a good selection of flowers, stems and leaves – the stems need not necessarily belong to the flowers: they can be arranged to look as if they do! It is helpful to arrange the design on a plain surface beside you until you are happy with it. The design in the photograph is overlaid and the ribbon 'tied round' the stems to look like a bunch of flowers is actually to hide the joins.

2  Turn each cutout face down on the pasting board and brush the glue evenly all over. The craft knife will be useful to lift them right side up again and to position the pieces on the washstand. Paste the underneath cutouts first and build up the decoration until it is balanced and lifelike. Press out the excess glue and air bubbles with your fingers, wipe glue off with kitchen paper, and when the cutouts are flat, press the edges down.

3  When the decoration is complete, leave it to dry, then clean up the surface of the work with a damp sponge or kitchen paper.

### • finishing •

Apply varnish as described on pages 13–14.

*JUG, BOWL, CHAMBERPOT AND MUG These tinware items make ideal accessories for your washstand. Prepare them all as described on pages 15–18. When the red oxide is dry, apply at least two coats of white primer undercoat letting it dry between coats. For the top coat apply two coats of white vinyl silk emulsion letting it dry between coats. Sponge in exactly the same way as the washstand using the remaining glaze. The insides of the accessories may be painted in plain blue or white. Decorate with delicate sprigs using the same paper as the washstand. Apply an antique gold finish to rims, handles, etc as described on page 13. Let it dry, then varnish as before*

# 11
# THE MODERN NURSERY

*I*n today's smaller homes space is at a premium and few children are fortunate enough to have a separate nursery. Many have their own bedroom though, and the designs in this chapter will help to create a pretty and functional room in which children can spend their earliest years.

• • • •

## TOY-BOX WITH CLOWN DECORATION

*Storage space for toys, etc is essential to any nursery. An old bathroom linen-box-cum-seat, bought very cheaply, has been painted in bright colours and decorated in a simple, well-spaced design using birthday wrapping paper. I could not resist the clowns on this pretty turquoise background and decided to paint the box the same colour. Luckily I found exactly the same shade in the Dulux range.*

┌─────────────────────────────────────────────────────────────────────┐

• *materials list* •

**LARGE BOX WITH LID**
**PREPARATION**
100 grade sandpaper
**PAINTING**
Small tin of white acrylic primer undercoat
2 sample pots of emulsion in colours of your choice, one for the outside and a contrast for inside
2.5cm (1 inch) brush
**DÉCOUPAGE**
3 sheets of paper with a clown motif
1 sheet of paper for cutting into borders

Small sharp scissors
Craft knife
Wallpaper paste
Glue brush • Pasting board
Small sponge or kitchen paper
**VARNISHING**
Takcloth
Small tin of semi-matt varnish or polyurethane lacquer
2.5cm (1 inch) brush
Fine-grade sandpaper
White spirit

└─────────────────────────────────────────────────────────────────────┘

► *CUT A DESIGN from birthday wrapping paper to decorate the nursery or children's room*

•

TOY-BOX *with clown decoration. This bright, cheerful piece is ideal for any nursery or playroom*

### ◆ *preparation* ◆

1 Sand down the old painted surface to form a 'key' on which to paint.

2 Remove dust and apply two or three coats of white undercoat, allowing to dry between coats. Prop the lid up to avoid sticking while the paint dries. Paint the inside also.

3 Apply two or three coats of a top colour to match

◆

your décor, letting it dry between coats. When the inside undercoat is dry, paint on the contrasting colour. Leave the lid open and allow to dry.

### ◆ *découpage* ◆

As you can see in the photograph it was impossible to eliminate many of the 'HAPPY BIRTHDAY' letters, but it doesn't seem to detract from the overall decoration.

1　Cut the borders first and stick them on, making the necessary adjustments at the corners to prevent creasing. Cut a large pile of clowns and a lot of extra balloons and bits and bobs to fill in. Aim to decorate the box on all sides and on the top as well as inside the lid.

2　Turn each cutout face down on to the pasting board and brush the paste evenly over the surface ensuring the edges are covered. Turn the cutouts right side up and stick on to the surface, gently pressing out excess glue and air bubbles with a rolling finger movement working from the centre outwards. Wipe away glue with damp kitchen paper. You will find the craft knife useful for lifting the more delicate pieces from the pasting board and altering their position on the surface of the box. When you are satisfied that each cutout is flat, press down the edges. Continue in this way until the box is decorated, remembering to stand back and take stock occasionally.

3　Leave the work to dry before cleaning up the surface with a damp sponge or kitchen paper.

### ◆ *finishing* ◆

Varnish the box as described on pages 13–14.

*ROCKING-HORSE STOOL*
*Rocking horses brighten up*
*an old stool which was*
*prepared and painted in the*
*same way as the toy-box. It*
*is decorated with rocking*
*horses cut from the border-*
*type paper with colourful*
*strips on the legs*

# DINOSAUR TRUNK

*After the hype of* Jurassic Park *and the expensive merchandise it created here is a unique (and cheap)
alternative. Children will appreciate the lovable dinosaurs which decorate their brightly painted tin trunk and it
will be particularly special to them as you will have made it.*
*Old travelling trunks are easily found, but it is most important to be sure that when the lid is up, it stays up
and will not fall shut on to small fingers. There must be a stay on one side of the lid inside the trunk which
locks straight once the lid is up and has to be physically bent again before the lid will close. Choose a vibrant
fun colour and a contrasting one for the trimmings – any child will love it!*

*THIS TRUNK provides* Jurassic Park *style as a low-budget feature*

---

## ◆ *materials list* ◆

**LARGE BOX WITH HINGED LID AND SAFETY STAY**

**PREPARATION**

If your trunk is metal: small tin of red oxide
    metal primer

2.5cm (1 inch) brush

White spirit

If your trunk is wooden: 100 grade sandpaper

**PAINTING**

Small tin of white acrylic primer undercoat

2 × 250ml tins of bright colour emulsion (one
    for inside, one for outside)

Sample pot of vibrant contrasting emulsion for
    trimmings

2.5cm (1 inch) brush

No. 8 artist's brush

**DÉCOUPAGE**

3 sheets of good quality wrapping paper or
    birthday paper

Small sharp scissors

Craft knife

Wallpaper paste

Glue brush   ◆   Pasting board

Small sponge or kitchen paper

**VARNISHING**

Takcloth

Small tin semi-matt varnish or polyurethane
    lacquer

2.5cm (1 inch) brush

White spirit

## ◆ *preparation* ◆

1  If your trunk is metal, prepare as described on pages 15–18. If wooden, sand with 100 grade sandpaper to provide a key for the paintwork.

2  Lift the trunk up on to a working-height surface. Apply two or three coats of white acrylic primer undercoat until the surface looks perfect. Allow paint to dry between coats. Paint on two or three coats of the top colour – walk around it to check that every nook and cranny has been painted. When it is dry remember to turn it upside down to paint underneath!

3  Paint the inside last taking care with the top edge (when the lid is shut the contrasting inside colour should not be visible). Leave the lid open and allow to dry.

## ◆ *découpage* ◆

1  Cut out a good selection of dinosaurs, balloons and other little items to fill in.

2  Turn each cutout face down on to the pasting board

and apply the glue, brushing it evenly over the surface making sure the edges are covered. Use a craft knife to turn the cutouts right side up and place on to the surface of the trunk. Press out the excess glue and air bubbles with a rolling movement of the fingers until it is flat before pressing down the edges. Wipe excess glue off with damp kitchen roll. Stand back and look at the design occasionally to appreciate it overall.

3  When the decoration is finished, leave it to dry out before cleaning up the surface with dampened kitchen paper.

## ◆ *finishing* ◆

With very slightly thinned paint, and using the No. 8 artist's brush, paint around all the trimmings giving them three or four coats until the colour is dense. Prop the lid up a little to avoid sticking. Allow to dry; then varnish as described on pages 13–14.

# 12
# THE CONSERVATORY

*O*ld enamelware is ideal for the conservatory being both functional and decorative, perfect for displaying flowers and plants, carrying water and for extra storage.

A collection of Victorian and Edwardian tinware painted in dark country green sits comfortably on an old garden table standing in the undergrowth at the edge of the wood outside my house. The two exceptions are the travelling trunk which is black, decorated with huge pink peonies and white blossom, and the old pail which is painted in buttermilk with a simple design of hand-painted green leaves in swags with an antique gold rope design which twists around the bucket. Each piece is functional as well as decorative, perfect for displaying flowers, carrying water or for extra storage. Of special interest is the little hand-painted vasculum with honeysuckle, butterflies and other insects, used for collecting and carrying botanical samples or seeds.

▶ *OLD enamelware revamped*

# HALF-LIDDED WATER CAN

*A sweet little Edwardian hot-water can which has been painted in a rich dark green and decorated with a single spray of pink roses. The handle has hand-painted gold leaves on it and the outer rims and handle have been picked out in gold. The cutting for this project has to be absolutely meticulous! The paper is hand-painted and therefore once the work is under several layers of varnish it really does appear to be painted on the can.*

## • materials list •

**HALF-LIDDED WATER CAN or similar piece**

**PREPARATION**

Small tin of red oxide metal primer

An old 2.5cm (1 inch) brush

White spirit

**PAINTING**

250ml tin of very dark green vinyl matt or
 small vinyl silk emulsion

2.5cm (1 inch) or smaller brush

**DÉCOUPAGE**

Good quality hand-painted wrapping paper
 with sprays of roses

Small sharp scissors

Craft knife

Wallpaper paste

Glue brush

Pasting board

Small sponge or kitchen paper

**ANTIQUE GOLD**

Small tubes of Gold and Raw Umber artists'
 acrylics

No. 4 artist's brush

Lidded container or jar

Water to mix

**VARNISHING**

Takcloth

Small tin of semi-matt varnish or polyurethane
 lacquer

2.5cm (1 inch) brush

## • preparation •

1  Prepare the can as described on pages 15–18.
2  When the red oxide is completely dry, apply three coats of dark green emulsion paint to ensure good dense coverage. By turning the can upside down to apply the second coat no small part of the surface will be left unpainted. Prop the lid open a little to avoid sticking and leave paint to dry between coats. Push the end of the brush into the spout and check that the inside of the handle is painted. When you are satisfied with the surface, leave to dry.

## • découpage •

1  Select blooms for their colour and shape to decorate the sides and the top of the can. Cut out each spray with great care: first cut the fine inside stems by making an initial incision with the scissor points; this gives you plenty of paper to hold. Cut the outer stems, etc last. Try not to remove any of the thorns as they look wonderful against the dark background, and remember to serrate the edges of the leaves.

If you have difficulty with long curling stems, cut them into sections and butt them together when you stick them on to the surface of the can; the joins will not be noticeable.
2  Turn each cutout singly face down on to the pasting board and apply the glue evenly brushing it out over the edges to ensure they are covered. Use a craft knife to lift delicate curling stems from the board and for positioning on the can. Work out any air bubbles and excess glue with your fingers and wipe it off carefully with damp kitchen paper. When the surface is flat press down the edges. Rinse fingers frequently as the glue will remove the surface from the paper.
3  When the design is complete let it dry. Using a damp sponge or kitchen paper, remove the glue from the background and surface of the work being careful not to scuff the edges. Leave to dry.

## • finishing •

Apply an antique gold finish to the rim and small handle as described on page 13. Using the same paint, decorate the large handle with leaves as described on page 22. Leave to dry, then varnish as described on pages 13–14.

▶ *THE SIMPLICITY of this decoration is most effective*

# 'PRETTY AS A PITCHER'

*Lovely old Victorian and Edwardian swan-neck pitchers, in their time known also as 'ewers', are becoming difficult to find. This is a pity as they are highly decorative and most useful. They can sometimes be found at car boot sales, jumble sales and in antique markets – ask a dealer to look out for one.*
*Pitchers have great decorative potential, and look delightful painted in black, traditional dark green or paint-finished in parchment or pastel colours.*

## • materials list •

**SWAN-NECK PITCHER**
**PREPARATION**
Small tin of red oxide metal primer
2.5cm (1 inch) brush
White spirit
Kitchen paper
**PAINTING**
250ml tin of emulsion in the colour of your
  choice
2.5cm (1 inch) brush
**DÉCOUPAGE**
Floral wrapping paper
Small sharp scissors
Craft knife
Wallpaper paste
Glue brush   •   Pasting board
Small sponge or kitchen paper
**ANTIQUE GOLD**
Tubes of Gold and Raw Umber artists' acrylics
No. 4 or 5 artist's brush
Lidded container or jar
Water to mix
**VARNISHING**
Takcloth
Small tin of semi-matt varnish or polyurethane
  lacquer
2.5cm (1 inch) brush
White spirit

## • preparation •

1   Prepare the jug as instructed on pages 15–18.
2   With your hand inside it, apply the first coat of paint to the inside of the handle and the outer surface. Stand the jug upside down and paint the base. Leave to dry. Hold by the handle for the second coat and paint inside as far as the neck seam. Leave to dry. Three coats will be necessary to ensure adequate coverage.
3   If you have used a cream topcoat you may wish to apply a parchment paint-finish at this stage (see page 20).

## • découpage •

1   Cut out a good selection of flowers, leaves, etc.
2   Turn each cutout face down on to the pasting board and brush on the glue evenly, ensuring that the edges are covered. Lift with a craft knife and position on the jug. Press gently, working out excess glue and air bubbles with your fingers until the paper is flat. Press down the edges and wipe away excess glue with damp kitchen paper.
3   When the decoration is finished and the glue has dried, clean up the surface of the paper and background with damp kitchen paper. Leave to dry.

## • finishing •

Apply an antique gold finish to the rims of the jug as described on page 13 and leave to dry. Then varnish as instructed on pages 13–14, being careful to avoid dribbles from the base of the handle and around the top rim. All the jugs in the photographs have at least 10 coats of varnish.

▶ *IVY AND OLD roses look lovely on either background*

SOPHISTICATED TALL black
Victorian and Edwardian
swan-necked pitchers which
have been elaborately
decorated and gilded stand
alongside an early nineteenth-
century tin hatbox
hand-painted with dog roses
by the author

# FLORAL PLANTERS

*In this section you will find three planters, initially similar (though of varying size) but all quite different now they are decorated. The largest is painted in black with a simple decoration of nasturtiums, very vibrant and sophisticated, photographed with red cyclamen.*

*BRILLIANT RED cyclamen complement this design beautifully*

◆

## materials list

**METAL PLANTER**

**PREPARATION**
Small tin of red oxide primer
An old 2.5cm (1 inch) brush
White spirit
Kitchen paper

**PAINTING**
250ml tin of black vinyl matt or small vinyl silk
   emulsion
2.5cm (1 inch) brush

**DÉCOUPAGE**
Wrapping paper with nasturtium motif
Small sharp scissors
Craft knife
Wallpaper adhesive
Glue brush
Pasting board
Small sponge or kitchen paper
Piece of white chalk

**ANTIQUE GOLD**
Tubes of Gold and Raw Umber artists'
   acrylics
No. 5 artist's brush
Lidded container or jar
Water to mix

**VARNISHING**
Takcloth
Small tin of semi-matt varnish or polyurethane
   lacquer
2.5cm (1 inch) brush

**FINAL TOUCHES**
Small amount of self-adhesive suede or baize
   for base
Kitchen scissors

## preparation

1   Prepare the planter as described on pages 15–18.
2   When the red oxide is dry, apply at least three coats of black emulsion to all surfaces of the planter, allowing the paint to dry between coats.

## découpage

1   Cut the nasturtiums and their curling stems meticulously as the colour contrast against the black will be a knock-out and untidy cutting very obvious! If you find the stems difficult, cut them into sections and butt them together when you stick them to the surface; it will not be noticeable. You may find it helpful to turn the planter on its side and lay the design on it to get an idea of how it will look. Draw around the flowers and stems with chalk, marking out their shape: this will be a good guide when you place the delicate pasted stems into position.
2   Turn each cutout singly face down on to the pasting board and brush on the glue evenly all over the surface. Lift from the board with a craft knife, turn right side up (do not panic when it curls up) and stick to the planter by pressing very gently with a rolling movement of the fingers, working out the excess glue which can be removed with kitchen paper. When the air bubbles are pressed out and the surface is flat, press down the edges. (*NOTE*  When working with fine stems it is important to keep fingers clean otherwise the surface of the paper will stick to them and will be ruined.)
3   When the decoration is complete leave it to dry. Clean up the work, removing dried glue, etc from the background and decoration with a damp sponge or kitchen roll. Leave to dry.

## finishing

Apply an antique gold finish to the top rim as described on page 13, ensuring a neat finish on the inside also. Leave to dry, then varnish as described on pages 13–14. The inside of the planter will require about two coats.

## final touches

Cut a piece of self-adhesive suede or baize to shape and stick to the bottom of the planter to protect furniture, and give a professional finish.

 HERE IS THE BLACK PLANTER AGAIN, *this time photographed in a huge Victorian conservatory
with the harvest of summer gathered in and piled around it. The nasturtiums are actually
growing up through the garden table!*

# ROSE PLANTER

ROSES DECORATE *a Soft Ochre paint-finished background on a
medium-sized planter which has a soft brown paint on the
inside to add a little contrast. Follow all the guidelines for the
previous planter, varying the colour of the topcoat of paint. A
three-colour sponge finish has been applied in Yellow Ochre,
Chinese White and Cadmium Yellow artists' acrylics using the
technique described on pages 19–20.*

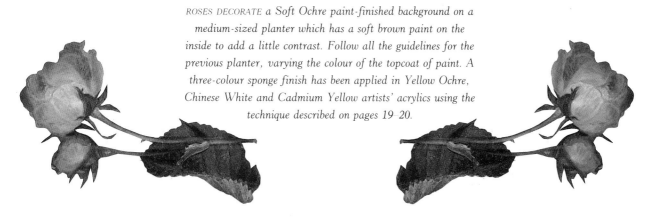

# ROSEBUD PLANTER

FADED OLD ROSEBUDS *on twisted ribbons are a simple and*
*pretty adornment for the smallest planter. This one is painted*
*in dark umbery-green outside and a strong Cayenne inside.*

# RIBBONS AND ROSES PLANTER

*SWAGS, RIBBONS AND ROSES adorn this planter which is an old enamel washing bowl rejuvenated with spring-green paint on the outside and cream inside sponged directly from the tin with the same green.*

# 13
# UNUSUAL ANTIQUES

Throughout this final chapter you will find several of my favourite objects with which I am now unable to part.

I hope that they will both inspire you and demonstrate to you the incredible diversity of objects there are to decorate and the many interesting possibilities and ideas which present themselves afresh with each new project.

Three of these (the hatbox, the nutmeg tin and the ham boiler) are decorated with identical paper, although not the same flowers, and the background colours crop up more than once. The overall theme is 'swags, ribbons and roses'. I do hope you will enjoy looking through them and that you will be fired with enthusiasm to collect a few unusual (and cheap) antiques. Good hunting.

• • • •

▶ HATBOX *This charming nineteenth-century tin hatbox in perfect condition has been given the 'swags, ribbons and roses' treatment. A dear friend of mine, Marianne Grace, decorated it using the same paper as the enamel bowl planter on page 133, choosing the open blooms and spacing them out singly into deep swags. The roses on the lid have a hand-painted twisted ribbon running through them.*

*Old hatboxes can still be found in antique markets or shops specializing in tinwear, though rarely in this pristine condition. Have you looked in your attic lately?*

*The hatbox was prepared as described on pages 15–18, painted in a dark umbery-green vinyl silk emulsion and gilded **after** varnishing with liquid gold*

# DOMED TRUNK

DOMED TRUNK *Isn't this 'darling' → a little Victorian trunk in
such a lovely shape. Unusually, it still has its padlock. I felt
that it should be a very feminine piece and therefore painted
it in this delightful soft turquoise and decorated it with
violas cut from a paper which depicts French textiles. I am
thrilled with the result, especially as I have never come
across another like it.*

# NUTMEG TIN

NUTMEG TIN *The tin is divided into sections inside with a circular grater in the centre. Prepared as usual for tinware (pages 15–18) and decorated with poppies and roses on a deep sea-green background with hand-painted gold leaves. Very simple to do and a stunning little object.*

# HAM BOILER

*HAM BOILER* Rounder *than a fish kettle, the old ham boiler is a lovely oval shape with a domed lid. The moment I spotted it I visualized it decorated in a regency style. You may recognize both the paper and background paint from earlier projects. I think the gorgeous turquoise and delicate roses look perfect.*

*I adore this gift-wrap paper which depicts nineteenth-century floral French textiles; all very different but ideal for découpage (see suppliers list on page 142). The paper is extremely thin and requires careful cutting and pasting but, as you see, the end result is well worth the trouble.*

# MAIL TRAY

*MAIL PRESENTATION TRAY* This metal tray was prepared as
usual for tinware (see pages 15–18), then painted dark
country-green with a simple design of rose stems. As the handle
is brass the plate was left ungilded.

# VICTORIAN FOOTWARMER

VICTORIAN FOOTWARMER *This is the sweetest thing and would originally have been in plain metal, filled with hot water and slipped under the cushion of a Victorian footstool. It was prepared as usual for tinware (see pages 15–18), and painted in black vinyl silk emulsion before applying the découpage decoration of water lilies complete with kingfisher. The leaves are hand-painted in antique gold acrylics.*

# ACKNOWLEDGEMENTS

Thanks to the following for making this book possible: Virginia Hiller for suggesting I write a book in the first place, and for introducing me to Di Lewis. Di Lewis for her wonderfully inspired photography throughout the book; it has been both a privilege and a pleasure to work with her and I have gained much from her experienced eye and professional guidance; she has inspired and encouraged me with her ideas, enthusiasm and drive and I value her continued friendship. Polly Mobsby of Smart Arts for her kindness and patience in allowing us to photograph in her lovely home and grounds on countless occasions and for supplying textiles, antiques and props. Marianne Grace, a fine artist, gardener and dear friend, for her beautiful artwork in the book, her calm countenance and sense of humour and her inspirational ideas, many of them incorporated in this book. Vivienne Wells and Brenda Morrison at David & Charles for their trust in a novice, allowing me to get on with the book without pressure; for their encouragement and support throughout. Marianne and Peter Methley for allowing us to photograph in their beautiful home and Lizzie and Simon Smith for letting us photograph their gorgeous children, Annabel and Charlie, for the nursery project. Terry 'Whoosh' Penny of Smart Arts for making all the screens in the book and the unusually shaped bedhead in the shortest possible time. Caspari Ltd, National Gallery Publications Ltd and Jemima Haddock of Alan Hutchison Limited, all of whom generously supplied their wonderful papers. Sandra Wall-Armitage, a skilful botanical artist and teacher, whose deep love of flowers shows in her work. Her beautiful papers are used often throughout the book and were certainly a challenge and a true test of cutting! (I have tried hard to find the owners of all the papers used. Where this has not been possible please accept my apologies.) Laura Ashley Ltd for supplying their lovely rich red 'Aragon' fabric for the photographs on page 90. Ken Haskell, head gardener extraordinaire, for his fabulous roses on page 75 and Nina Lockyer for the variegated leaves and flowers from her garden. Finally, many thanks and love to my family and friends for their constant help and support.

◆

# GUIDE TO SUPPLIERS

### • *papers* •

Harry N. Abrams Inc
100 Fifth Avenue
New York
NY 10011
Telephone (+1) 212 206 7715

Harry N. Abrams Inc
PO Box 34
2110 AA Aerdenhut
Netherlands
Telephone (+31) 23 249031
UK Distributors:
Thames And Hudson Ltd
30–34 Bloomsbury Street
London WC1B 3QP
Telephone: 0171 636 5488
Giftwraps by artists; French flowers; nineteenth-century textile designs

Caspari Ltd
9 Shire Hill
Saffron Walden
Essex CB11 3AP
Telephone 01799 513010
Fax 01799 513101

Dover Publications Inc
31 East 2nd Street
Mineola
NY 11501
UK Distributors:
Constable Publishers
3 The Lanchesters
162 Fulham Palace Road
London W6 9ER
Telephone 0181 741 3663
and

The Dover Bookshop
18 Earlham Street
London WC2H 9LN
(mail order service; catalogue on request)
Books of giftwrap including Redoute roses (three sizes), floral, Chinese floral, old fashioned Christmas etc and the Dover pictorial archives series

Alan Hutchison Ltd
9 Pembridge Studios
27A Pembridge Villas
London W11 3EP
Telephone 0171 221 0129
Fax 0171 229 0829

Henry Ling and Son Ltd
Chiddingstoke Causeway
Nr Tonbridge
Kent TN11 8JP
Telephone 01892 870333
Hand-painted papers by Sandra Wall-Armitage

National Gallery Publications Ltd
5/6 Pall Mall East
London SW1Y 5BA
Telephone 0171 839 8544

### • *decorating tools and materials* •

Craig and Rose plc
172 Leith Walk
Edinburgh EH 5EB
Telephone 0131 554 1131
Extra pale dead-flat varnish, goldsize, gold leaf, specialist brushes, etc. Paint manufacturers with stockists nationwide

Farrow and Ball
33 Uddens Trading Estate
Uddens Cross, Wimborne
Dorset BH21 7NL
Telephone 01202 876141

Sole manufacturers and suppliers of the National Trust range of paints, etc used on National Trust properties. These paints are available by mail order in a range of subtle, rich, dusky colours. There are seven types of paint in the range which can be used along the same lines as modern paints. There is also an old-fashioned dead-flat oil, which has a lovely deep matt finish; an oil-bound distemper and soft distemper used for internal plasterwork and ceilings. Primers and undercoats are also available and the loveliest traditionally made wallpaper – real faded elegance! The paints are available by mail order only

Green and Stone
259 King's Road
London SW3 5ER
Telephone 0171 352 0837
also at:
1 North House
North Street
Chichester
Sussex PO19 1LR
Telephone 01243 533953
Suppliers of Pebeo crackling and ageing varnish and le Franc and Bourgeois crackling and ageing varnishes. Artists' materials, specialist brushes, acrylic varnish, powder colours, shellac, stencilling materials, etc

John Myland Ltd
80 Norwood High Street
London SE27 9NW
Telephone 0171 670 9161
Stockists of artist's brushes, the takcloths, many oil-based varnishes and polyurethane lacquers, shellac, universal stainers, gedgewax polish and a huge range of beeswax polishes, liming wax, goldsize, emulsions including earth colours, and much more. Mail order service

E. Ploton (Sundries) Ltd
273 Archway Road
London N6 5AA
Telephone 0181 348 2838
Artists' materials, artists' acrylics, oil paints, crackle varnish, specialist brushes and much more. Mail order service

## • *unpainted items* •

(Please telephone first to ascertain opening hours)

Acres Farm
Bradfield
Reading
Berkshire RG7 6JH
Telephone 01734 744305/744162
Fax 01734 744012
Candleshades, candlesticks, brass followers, etc

Cobwebs
Fordingbridge Road
Alderholt
Nr Fordingbridge
Hampshire
Telephone 01425 656534
Country antiques and second-hand furniture to paint and refurbish, old enamel and tinware, linen, pine, etc

Rubena Grigg
Hand-painted Furniture and Découpage
Telegraph Cottage
Cranborne
Dorset BH21 5QU
Telephone 01725 517826
Screens (large and small), fireboards, bed headboards in various shapes and sizes, coffee tables, wine bottle coasters, octagonal tablemats, etc all in MDF, made to order. Training and tuition available, commissions undertaken

Smart Arts
1 High Street
Fordingbridge
Hampshire SP6 1AS
Telephone 01425 655520
Well worth a visit for country antiques, pine furniture, antique textiles and linen and lace, porcelain, gifts, etc

'Squirrels'
Lyndhurst Road
Brockenhurst
Hampshire
Telephone 01590 22433
Lovely porcelain and antique pine

# INDEX